S0-BEF-834

'The modern architectural drawing is interesting, the photograph is magnificent, the building is an unfortunate but necessary stage between the two.'
H.S. Goodhart-Rendel, President of the RIBA, 1937-1939

Published in association with
The Royal Institute of British Architects
Drawings Collection

David Dean

Architecture of the 1930s

Recalling the English Scene

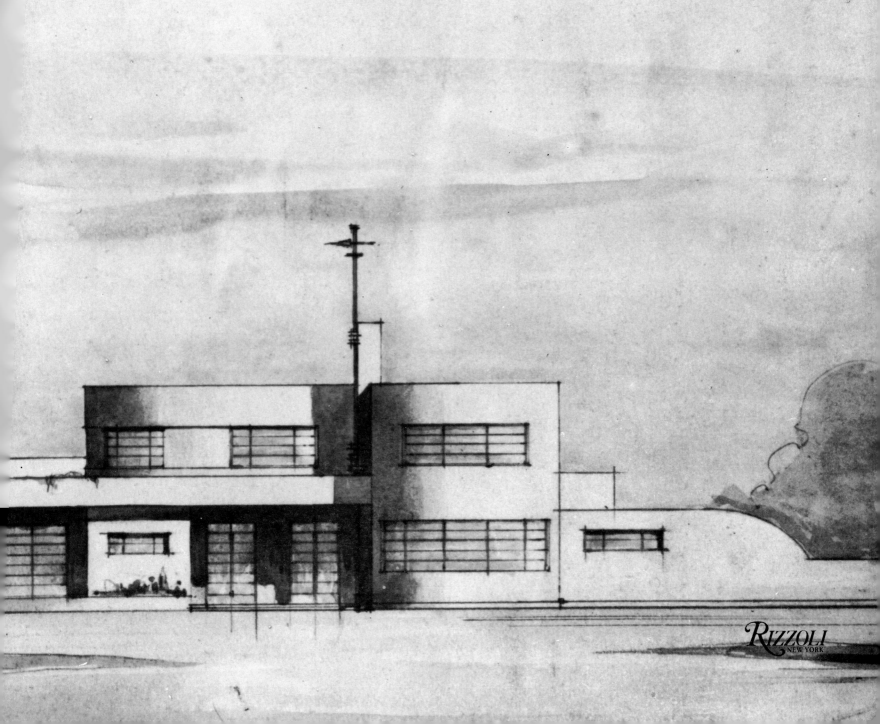

RIZZOLI
NEW YORK

Foreword

Published in the United States of America in 1983 by
Rizzoli International Publications, Inc.
712 Fifth Avenue, New York, NY 10019
First published in Great Britain by Trefoil Books Ltd.

Copyright © David Dean

All rights reserved. No part of this publication
may be reproduced, stored in any retrieval system, or transmitted in any
form or by any means, electronic, mechanical, photocopying or
otherwise, without the prior permission in writing of the publishers.

The publishers wish to acknowledge the generous support of the
Headley Trust in the preparation and production of this book.

ISBN 0 8478 0485 2 (paperback)
ISBN 0 8478 0484 4 (cloth)

Set by Words & Pictures Ltd. London
Printed in Hungary

The Royal Institute of British Architects is very proud to be the custodian of its incomparable British Architectural Library, of which the Drawings Collection forms an important part. In scope the Collection is the largest and most comprehensive body of architectural designs in the world, with a quarter of a million drawings from the Renaissance to the present day. It is naturally orientated towards British drawings, great numbers of them presented by the architects themselves, but it contains also some magnificent continental groups, notably the Drummond Stewart collection of baroque theatre designs and the Burlington Devonshire collection which includes almost all the surviving drawings of Palladio, perhaps the most influential architect in history.

The Collection is exhaustively organised, but the use made of it by the whole international community imposes very considerable pressures on the RIBA, for published catalogues are of necessity costly. I was delighted, therefore, when the Headley Trust asked us to find a way to produce a number of illustrated books to make the treasures of the Collection known to a wider public, and to follow this by travelling exhibitions on some of the themes selected.

The fruit of this enlightened patronage is the present series of substantially illustrated books, each supported by a scholarly text, on widely different aspects of the Collection. I am confident that they will give as much pleasure to others as they have given to me.

Owen Luder
President, Royal Institute of British Architects

Contents

ROYAL ACADEMY OF ARTS,
PICCADILLY, LONDON, W1V 0DS

Telephone: 01-734 9052
Cables: Royacad, London

The RIBA's 30s Exhibition in 1979 opened with a special reunion party for
those who had "been there". This sketch is Sir Hugh Casson's apology for not
attending

Preface and Acknowledgements

My gratitude is due first of all to the actors in the drama themselves, whose graphic and written records abound in the RIBA's British Architectural Library. Survivors of the period have been generous in discussion and in enduring my questions; and the full roll of those, of whatever generation, to whom I am indebted would be too long to call. Indeed many may have been unaware that they were adding pieces to my jigsaw, and certainly they bear no responsibility for any judgements made in what follows.

For a great range of help I must record my thanks to G.R. Adams; J.B. Bamborough; Sir John Betjeman; Colin Boyne; the Hon. Mrs Victor Bruce; R.A. Bullivant; Bertram Carter; E.J. (Bobby) Carter; Sir Hugh Casson (who allowed me to use the sketch on the facing page); William Crabtree; John B. Denman; Professor Gerald Dix; Maxwell Fry; Ernö Goldfinger; Gontran Goulden; John Grigg; Christopher and Anthea Holme (who read my manuscript and made valuable comments); Edward Mendelson; Leonard Miall; Richard and Chlöe Musman; Lord Reilly; Sir James Richards; Paul Rotha; Matthew Saunders; Gavin Stamp; Sir John Summerson; V. West (Works Manager, Cumberland Hotel); and Miriam Wornum. I am grateful too to the photographer Geremy Butler for his patience and skill.

My colleagues have applied the goad with enthusiasm. I have had particular help from Margaret Richardson, Jill Lever and Sally Dale, and I owe a special debt to the two colleagues who helped me to organise the RIBA's 1979 *Unlocking the Thirties* exhibition, Jane Preger and Robert Elwall. The latter's tireless assiduity in hunting out material for that occasion produced results which have been invaluable to me.

Acknowledgements are due to Messrs Faber, Country Life and the Architectural Press for permission to reproduce copyright material, and to Jane Ridley for allowing me to quote from her great-grandfather Sir Edwin Lutyens' letters. Finally, I have used a number of admirable contemporary photographs from the BAL's collection, and it has not always been possible to trace the original photographers. Their work has done much to amplify my illustrations, and I hope they will accept this expression of my gratitude.

In 1979 the British Architectural Library of the Royal Institute of British Architects mounted an exhibition on the 1930s in England, drawn from its own collections of drawings, contemporary photographs, manuscripts and architects' scrapbooks. Taking no partisan position, it displayed the extraordinary variety of the architectural scene, the traditional, the compromise, the uncompromising, the shops and pubs and private houses, the frock-coated public buildings and the fantasy world of the cinemas.

Within its restricted space it tried to suggest the ebullience of the age, to plunge back into it and show what it was really like in all its untidy vitality. What it could not do was to place the 30s in their wider social and cultural context, and that is part of the intention of the present scrapbook.

For scrapbook it is: not a rounded history, evaluating and docketing neatly away, but a presentation of the decade solely from contemporary sources. So there is much quotation, but all of it from those who were there, not from a later generation of critics. In effect it is an anthology in words and pictures, without hindsight or technicalities. The pictures have largely been left to tell their own story. The text sketches out a general view of 30s architecture and the soil from which it sprang as it looked at the time to the interested layman.

The material used comes almost entirely, and by deliberate choice, from the resources of the British Architectural Library, a good deal of it never before published. Inevitably, then, there are gaps; and conversely the space given to certain architects – Oliver Hill, Raymond McGrath, Oliver Bernard, for instance – is allotted not according to some yardstick of supposed importance but because the BAL has illuminating material on people, sometimes unjustly neglected, whose work strikingly evokes the period.

David Dean

Introduction

The whirligig of time has led some observers to look back on the 1930s with indulgent amusement. But to regard the period as merely chic is to insult it. Beyond question it was a brilliant age, even if some of its glitter came from tinsel. It identified real enemies, pursued with gusto exhilarating causes and extravagant passions, and had more than its share both of idealistic commitment and of fatuous complacency. And the stage on which the drama was played out was given a special poignancy by the final curtain which fell on September 3rd 1939.

Forty eight hours before Europe plummeted into the Second World War and on the very day Hitler's troops marched into Poland, W.H. Auden wrote (in a poem he later disowned) 'I sit in one of the dives/On Forty Second Street/Uncertain and afraid/As the clever hopes expire/Of a low dishonest decade.' He exactly caught the desolate realisation that time had finally run out ('Defenceless under the night/Our world in stupor lies'); but 'a low dishonest decade'? Such a judgement, coloured by the circumstances of his own life, is not acceptable as a verdict on the age itself.

In 1930 the First World War had been over only for a dozen years, and it was not for a full decade after the Armistice that the great war books began to appear: *Undertones of War* (1928), *Goodbye to All That* (1929), *All Quiet on the Western Front* (1929), *Memoirs of an Infantry Officer* (1930). Immediately after this half-way point between the two wars Japan invaded Manchuria, and the series of military aggressions (often called 'interventions') which were to lead to the next war was inexorably on course. The decade began with the first television transmission and ended with the New York World's Fair. Equally, it began with an unprecedented slump and ended with bewildered children being fitted for gasmasks.

Within this sombre frame is a profusion of images: the march from Jarrow and the road to Wigan Pier, house parties on the sunlit lawn, the burning of the Reichstag and the bombing of Guernica, endless fun, endless earnest colloquies on how to remake the world, hiking, biking and home to the bypass bijou – and out again for the weekly visit to the cinema's opulent darkness. And the *dramatis personae*: Orwell, Ivor Novello, Mrs. Simpson, Fred Perry and Malcolm Campbell, Priestley, J.D. Bernal and the brothers Huxley, Mosley, Lady Diana Duff Cooper, Roy Campbell's composite poet MacSpaunday – the list, which could go on for ever, shows how unclassifiably various life was. Wretched poverty faced outrageous privilege, and there was a ferment of question and rejection over society's received ideas by a generation just too young to have taken part in the war. The gulf was almost unbridgeable between those who could recall the long Edwardian sunshine and the young men born too late for the trenches and determined above all things not to allow control to drift back into the hands of the old, who had made such a mess of things last time. How these clashes were reflected in architecture is part of the theme of this book. But only part, for many capable and prosperous practitioners, neither radical in their views nor 'progressive' in their work, simply got on with the job largely untouched by the turmoil around them.

Its vigour, its inventiveness, its very copiousness, help to keep the 30s relevant. For the era still seems quite close; not a period buried in the past but one which still directly colours our lives. We can gauge its distance by returning to 1930 ourselves and looking back from that vantage point over much the same span, to 1880. Frank Lloyd Wright was a schoolboy then; Gaudi had just graduated. Gladstone was defeating Disraeli at the polls for the last time. Le Corbusier, Mies van der Rohe, Gropius were not yet born, nor was Picasso or J.M.Keynes or P.G. Wodehouse, nor, for that matter, Hitler or Mussolini. In their cradles in Austria and Georgia lay Albert Einstein and Josef Stalin; and an English architect named Forster had just become the father of a boy who was to be a distinguished novelist. How remote and irrelevant that age must have seemed to a young architect in 1930!

The nineteenth century had seen the overwhelming effects of the industrial revolution; huge population growth, the shift from country to town, a new mercantile class, a new proletariat. All this was soon to destroy the old stable dominance of aristocratic taste which had provided a tested building vocabulary from the mansion to the cottage. When the new century opened England was, briefly, a world architectural force. Parker and Unwin were pioneering the planning and design of low cost housing at Letchworth and Hampstead Garden Suburb. The Arts and Crafts Movement had given rise to some remarkable architects – Ashbee, Baillie Scott, Voysey, and, above all, Charles Rennie Mackintosh in Scotland – whose work aroused keen interest on the continent of Europe. The German architect Hermann Muthesius was seconded to the Imperial Embassy in London in 1896 to carry out major studies of the English house, and when he finally returned home in 1903 he took with him glowing and influential reports of what he had found.

But the dominance was not to last, and by the 20s no single manner had the strength to replace the standards which had been unquestioned a hundred years previously. By 1930 the new materials were there; the industrial and commercial needs were plain; homes fit for heroes had been promised; but the young modern architect found the instruction manuals dog-eared and almost comically out of date. He demanded a whole new vocabulary, founded on something more relevant than the tenets of Vitruvius and Palladio, the Greek or the Gothic. And to devise it must involve scrutiny of society's real needs and a sweeping away of preconception and cliché. In no earlier age could an architect have written, as Wells Coates did in *Unit One* (1934): 'Architecture has to serve the purposes of the people as well as the purposes of beauty.' By 1930 nothing could be taken for granted any more: so at least the modern architect thought.

The word Modern has lost most of the excitement it used to arouse in the 30s. By 1951, the year of the Festival of Britain, it had become a general descriptive term (and not a very useful one since 'modern architecture' had comprehensively swept the board). Twenty years later still, labels like Post-Modernism had arrived to kick the last life out of its 30s gusto. But in the 1930s to declare yourself modern was consciously to take a militant position and there was no shortage of enemies. Besides the reactionaries, there was a formidable alliance, of traditionalists who found the starkness and strangeness of modernism aesthetically, even morally, abhorrent, of people with a financial or an emotional vested interest in the conventional, of those who simply disliked what was on offer or who were very satisfied with things the way they were.

To them Modern was an emotive term, and the conventional were galled by the bland takeover bid of a younger generation implied in phrases like 'the modern mind' and 'the modern sensibility' used to describe their own habits of thought. Today, descendants of the anti-modernists have brought the word full circle, from war cry, through description, to a nudging code word to imply dismissive ridicule of everything the Modern Movement stood for.

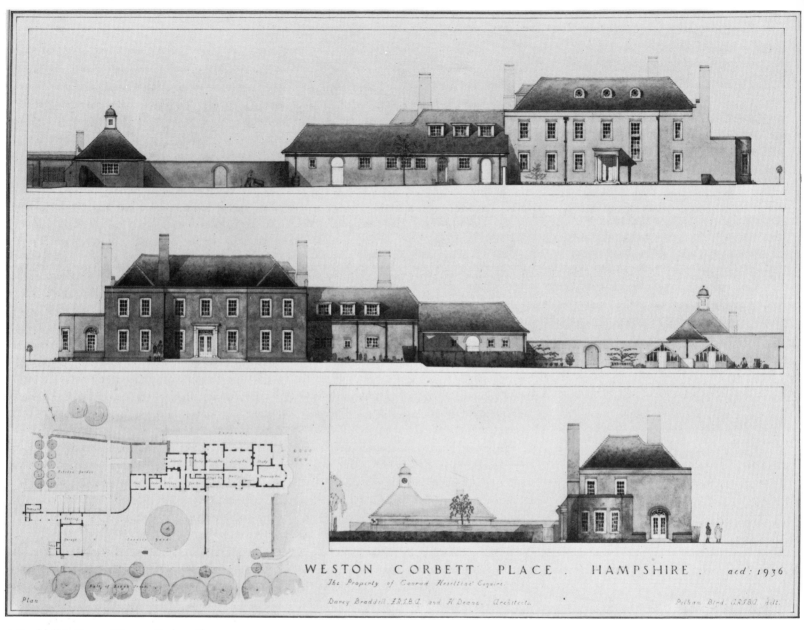

WESTON CORBETT PLACE . HAMPSHIRE . *acd: 1936*

The Property of Conrad Heseltine Esquire.

Darcy Braddell, F.R.I.B.A. and H. Deane, Architects.

Pelham Bird, A.R.I.B.A. del¹.

Plan

1 Braddell & Deane. Weston Corbett Place,
near Basingstoke. Plan & elevations. Pencil, pen
& watercolour (490 × 650)

Spec House and Country House

Many of the dominating figures in 30s building were not architects at all. They were speculative builders and commercial developers. Spec housing was decorated by, or had tacked onto it, a profusion of mostly unappealing motifs, from Neo-Tudor to the zigzag flashiness of Jazz Moderne, but these were only rarely drawn from the Modern Movement, whose images, even if wanted, were integral to the total design and not readily detachable. Spec work was often shoddy in character and greedy in motivation, and it heedlessly despoiled vast tracts of what had once beeen countryside, on the edge of towns, along the arterial roads (given importance by the newly popular recreation of motoring) and, notoriously, along the seacoast.

The Town and Country Planning Act of 1932 offered a potential for checking ribbon development and the wholesale wrecking of old towns for commercial exploitation. It wrote into the statute book such unlovely but useful phrases as 'likely seriously to injure the amenity of a locality', but it was little used against commercial greed. The protection of hitherto unspoiled country became an articulate middle-class cause, pioneered by such bodies as the Council for the Preservation of Rural England and the Design and Industries Association under the chairmanship of Clough Williams-Ellis (1883-1978). Architect of Portmeirion in North Wales, that triumphantly fanciful exercise in the placing of buildings in a landscape, he was more telling as author of *England and the Octopus* (1928), compiler of the vigorous DIA *Cautionary Guides* to places under threat, and tirelesss denouncer of sprawlingly uncontrolled advertisement hoardings. Dismay and disgust were widespread. They can be found even in such unlikely places as the catalogue to the RIBA's *Small House* exhibition of 1938. The exhibition was aimed at the layman, to encourage interest in good design in place of 'homes totally unworthy of their tradition...ruthlessly mutilating their countryside. Relentlessly, like an incurable skin disease, this unconsidered development creeps over the land.'

The great days of the substantial country house were over. Of course there were still traditional scholar-architects, and still prosperous clients who called on their services, but their numbers were dwindling. Weston Corbett Place, near Basingstoke, 1936 (fig. 1) by Darcy Braddell (1884-1970) and Humphry Deane, a house for Conrad Heseltine set in 400 acres, is an example of the sensitive houses which Braddell and Deane continued to design between the wars, utterly untouched by the turbulence of modernism around them.

Edward Maufe (1883-1974), best known for winning the Guildford Cathedral competition, also maintained a sizeable country house practice. Plate 1 shows the stylishly presented elevations and plans of his Yaffle Hill (1930) at Broadstone, near Poole, for his client C.C. Carter, probably Cyril Carter of Poole Potteries. The plan, symmetrical through a central axis, opens its arms to the sea and Maufe provides masses of vertical glazing on the seaward side. Unlike Braddell he did produce an essay in the modern manner four years later, a most untypical excursion, in his Round House at Poole Harbour, only a few miles from Yaffle Hill.

More modest in scale and more conventional in plan is the seemly Neo-Georgian White House at Bosham (1930) by Oswald P. Milne (1881-1968), (fig. 2) who had worked with both Sir Arthur Blomfield and Sir Edwin Lutyens. The Mayor of Hampstead and a cultivated figure, he was a friend of the poet and editor J.C. Squire, who had dedicated his *Essays on Poetry* to him and had founded, with his help, the Architecture Club in 1922.

Ashcombe Tower, near Dawlish in Devon (Plate 2) was designed in 1933-6 for Major Ralph Rayner MP by the New Zealander Brian O'Rorke (1901-1974). The garden front (fig. 3) is

2 Oswald P. Milne. The White House, Bosham

3 Brian O'Rorke. Ashcombe Tower, near Dawlish. Garden front

symmetrical; the main elevation is varied by a curiously massive and squat tower. The striking balustrade of the main staircase (fig. 4) hints at O'Rorke's other area of activity, for he was much involved, too, in interior design, particularly for ships, aircraft and trains. His most notable achievement here (see Plate III) is the work which the enlightened shipowner Colin Anderson commissioned from him for the liners of the Orient Steamship Navigation Company.

The most distinguished survivor from the great period of house design which had so impressed Muthesius at the outset of the century was C.F.A. Voysey (1857-1941). A letter from him to E.J. Carter, RIBA Librarian and Editor of the *RIBA Journal*, in the BAL files, and dated 21 October 1931, refers to H.M. Fletcher's 'kind and flattering review of my work' which had appeared in the *Journal* and goes on to make interesting comments on his clients and the houses he has built (fig. 5). The house he designed for his wife (and the only one he would care to live in) is The Orchard, Chorley Wood, Herts (1900).

4 Brian O'Rorke. Ashcombe Tower. The main staircase.

5 C.F.A. Voysey. Letter to E.J. Carter, 21 October 1931

I am sorry this article gives the impression that I did not consider my clients. As a matter of fact, out of 246 clients I have worked for 53 have returned with fresh commissions, & I have built 108 private houses only one of which I should care to live in, & that is the house I built for my wife.

13

Rumblings of Modernism

But of course the writing was on the wall for these spacious and untroubled country houses. Insistent rumours kept coming through of sensational happenings in Europe. The Modern Movement arrived very late in England. The first wave of it to catch the imagination came from Scandinavia and Holland, then from France with glimpses from Germany. Only the avant-garde grasped the full nature of what was happening, especially in Soviet Russia, though by the time that news got through, Stalinist Russia was already turning its back on post-revolutionary experiment in favour of the grimly monumental.

F.R. Yerbury's *Modern European Buildings* of 1928 included work by Mendelsohn from Germany, Dudok from Holland, Perret and Garnier from France (and Emberton from England), but nothing by Le Corbusier, Gropius or Mies van der Rohe. Four years later the architect Howard Robertson, more important as a propagandist than in his built work, published *Modern Architectural Design*, in which he illustrated roughly the same number of buildings each from Holland, Sweden and Germany, and twice as many from France. But there was still no Gropius.

The key book however had been published in England in 1927: Le Corbusier's *Vers une Architecture*, translated by Frederick Etchells (1887-1973). The translator himself is a highly interesting figure. Vorticist painter in Paris before the First World War, he turned to architecture in the 20s, designed, in the Crawford's building in Holborn, the first modern office building in England, founded Haslewood Books, a distinguished private press, and ended his career restoring churches in Berkshire.

Le Corbusier's book, with its sweep, its certainty and its incantatory fervour, was just what the young progressives had been waiting for. They were transfixed by its hymning of 'the great primary forms' of cube, cone, sphere, cylinder and pyramid and by its memorable dicta ('Architecture is the masterly, correct and magnificent play of masses brought together in light'). And his masterpiece, the Villa Savoye at Poissy (1928-9), was an irresistible icon. With this image always in their minds' eye of a slim white cube, lightly poised on stilts in a green field, there could be no doubt of the potency and, as it seemed, the definitive perfection of form which modern architecture could achieve in the new machine age.

Without even trying to master the doctrinal bases of the style (though style was not a word in the approved vocabulary), the progressive publicists of the early 30s could readily grasp and broadcast the metaphor of the machine. People expected their Electrolux vacuum cleaner and their Atco lawn mower to work. Their Morris Minor or Fraser Nash gave them trouble-free motoring, even if they did not know what went on under the bonnet. So they accepted, too, the concealed efficiency of the modern house, of everything under its lid. The working parts were taken for granted. What caught the imagination was the compelling image, clean, white, sharp, cutting sheer through the shambling picturesqueness, or the Hollywood razzmatazz, of their less enlightened fellows.

Emancipated from the sloppy and the random, from the furniture Granny left him, the Medici prints and the novels of A.J. Cronin ('let there be no Cronin at the bar', pleaded Cyril Connolly), emancipated in sober truth from what ordinary people thought of as homely and comfy, modern man saw himself keen-eyed, progressive, a natural leader. But it is unjust to mock. There may be cocktails on the sun terrace, with the *Architectural Review* (guide-book, totem, and art object) lying on the Breuer chair. Equally, there is profound concern about art education, ribbon development, the unemployed, slum clearance, and above all, drifting unchecked from Germany, the miasma of National Socialism, which was indeed to black out the decade.

The Modern House

Amyas Connell (1901-1980) was an early admirer of Le Corbusier. In 1924 he had worked his way to England on a tramp steamer with his fellow New Zealander Basil Ward (1902-1976) and they had been excited by Le Corbusier's Pavillon de l'Esprit Nouveau at the 1925 Paris Exposition des Arts Décoratifs. Both had then gone as prizewinners to the British School in Rome, and Connell's first commission was to design for the School's Director, Professor Bernard Ashmole, his inventive and assured house High and Over at Amersham in 1929. Alding (now New Farm) at Grayswood near Haslemere, Surrey (fig. 6) for Sir Arthur Lowes Dickinson followed in 1932, by which time Ward had become his partner. On a complex plan, radiating from a glazed stair tower, Alding shows Connell's concern for the play of light and shadow, voids and solids, and for bringing the continous windows flush with the external walls (and in practice doubling the fuel bills).

A year later the pair were joined by Colin Lucas (b.1906), who by the time he was 22, frustrated by conventional builders, had set up his own company to develop his ideas for reinforced concrete. Noah's House on the Thames at Bourne End (fig. 7), built for his family in 1930 for £1,150, was probably the first monolithic concrete house in England. Its fully glazed central living-room on the river front was flanked by five bedrooms. Figure 8 shows a group of three houses (two of them now extensively altered and the other demolished) which the new partnership designed at Saltdean near Brighton in 1934. Variations on a simple theme, with roof canopy and external stair to the sun terrace, these concrete houses, far from appearing poised like Corbusian white birds, seem like dice thrown out onto the landscape.

Stripped-down modern houses, besides running into trouble with planning committees, did not escape mockery. Goodhart-Rendel turned his urbane wit, so irksome to the solemn-minded, on them in 1932: 'One party yearns secretly for the vanished days when the Mistress Art gloried in the richness of her wardrobe; the other prefers the nude. With the nude, as an experienced

6 Amyas Connell. Alding (now New Farm), Grayswood, near Haslemere

7 Colin Lucas. Noah's House, near Bourne End.

8 Connell Ward & Lucas. Houses at Saltdean, near Brighton

Plate 1: Edward Maufe. Yaffle Hill, near
Broadstone. Plans & elevations: drawn by Evans
Palmer. Pencil & wash (630 × 480)

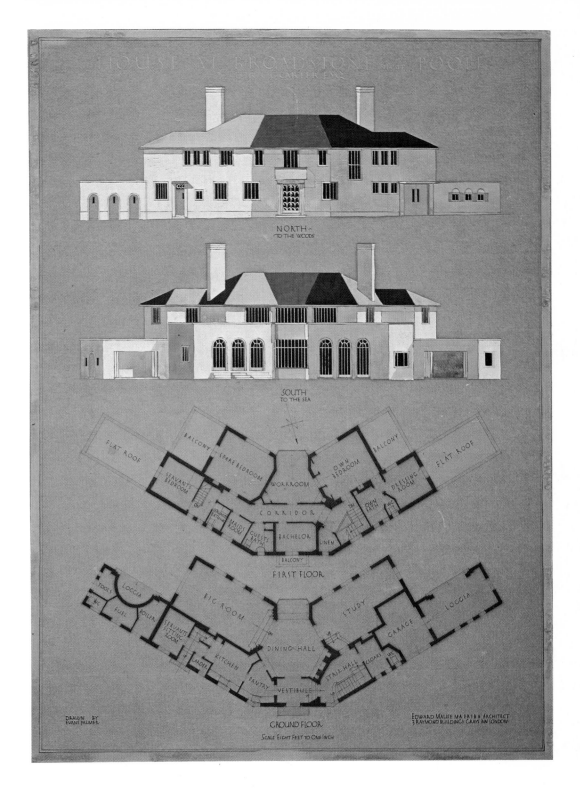

Plate 2: Brian O'Rorke. Ashcombe Tower, near
Dawlish. Perspective. Pencil & watercolour
(610 × 1300)

9 Paul Rotha. Cartoon, from the *Architectural Review*, September 1932

connoisseur said to me the other day. one knows the worst at once'. He was commenting on the entries for the RIBA Building competition (*Architect & Building News* 24 June 1932, p. 417), and he characteristically added: 'Most of the designs look very undressed indeed, and many of them it would have been a real kindness to cover up a little.'

Paul Rotha must have had Connell, Ward and Lucas in mind when he drew the cartoon which the *Architectural Review* published in September of the same year (fig. 9). Pioneer of the documentary film, Rotha, who worked with Ward on the RIBA's Film Committee, was to make in 1938 a spoof extravaganza for the British Commercial Gas Company called 'New Worlds for Old'. There was little money to hire professionals, and thirty of Rotha's friends, including Connell and Ward, had walk-on parts as stagedoor Johnnies and the like in a scene depicting night life in gas-lit Victorian London. The film ran into buffoonish trouble with the censors.

Another image, at the opposite extreme from that of the Modernists, was left over from Edwardian times as though the war had never happened. This was the vision of a contented hierarchical society, sustained by unquestioning respect. Landowner, parson, doctor, housemaid, gardener, all acted out their lives in an immemorial England, slumfree and utterly dependable. The myth was to reach its ripest expression in Hollywood's creation of the exquisite, touching and preposterous Mrs. Miniver. She would have been at home in Clobb Copse at Buckler's Hard in Hampshire, built for John Ehrmann in 1936-38, one of the last works of Baillie Scott (1865-1945). Figure 10 is his watercolour perspective of the garden front of this dateless brick house, half-timbered and tile-hung. Nowhere for Wells Coates to park his Lancia here.

A world away from Clobb Copse was the work of F.R.S. Yorke (1906-1962). In three highly influential books, *The Modern House* (1934), *The Modern House in England* (1937) and, with Frederick Gibberd, *The Modern Flat* (1937) he prescribed a coldly mechanistic view of architecture, based on

10 M.H. Baillie Scott. Clobb Copse, Buckler's Hard. Perspective of garden front. Watercolour (330 × 510)

Le Corbusier but quite lacking the lyrical and visionary philosophy that lay at the heart of the Corbusian aesthetic. The modernist made no attempt, said Yorke, 'to discover a new style or new shapes'; all, he implied, would come right if function was properly analysed and new materials and methods properly employed. Fortunately the evidence of the photographs in his books, most of them from the *Architectural Review*, showed enquirers that personal expression, elegance, beauty itself, had gone on doggedly finding a place in architecture.

Writing in 1967, Basil Ward was to say (D. Sharp *ed.: Planning and Architecture*, p.80) 'There could be no compromise for us. Beauty in architecture was manifest only when a unity of spatial and formal patterns based on the function of a building and the rightness of its structure was achieved.' But even so relentless a purist as Yorke came to realise that absolute doctrine could not be followed consistently. In *A Key to Modern Architecture* (1939), written with Colin Penn, he conceded that there was an initial 'tendency to over-emphasise the expression of structure, and pure functionalism was demanded at the expense of appearance...the strict functionalist is the puritan of architecture.' The abiding impression the reader derives from their book is not that the modern movement is simply one more chapter in the growth of architecture, but that it is moving towards a final perfection, which is indeed already in plain sight.

Yorke's Torilla, Nast Hyde, Hatfield (1934-5) for Mrs. Barbara Macdonald – figure 11 shows a preliminary scheme – has an austere rectilinear character whose oddly small windows take little advantage of the possibilities of the new materials. In the following year he took into partnership the emigré Hungarian architect Marcel Breuer (1902-1981), who had been working at the Bauhaus under Walter Gropius, preeminently as a designer of furniture in tubular steel, and later in bent plywood. Together Yorke and Breuer designed, again in concrete, Shangri-La at Lee-on-Solent (1936-7) for Hugh Rose (fig. 12). Like Torilla it employed the Corbusian motif of a living room rising through two storeys. The photograph of the south front (fig. 13), with its familiar outside cantilevered staircase, shows that by this time the severity of the doctrinaire Yorke is softened, without being compromised, by the first floor window grid above the living room and the external trellising which echoes it; and the free-form pool in the garden provides another humanising note.

Though the early modernists were committed to Cubist forms, there was an increasing, if covert, agreement to admit non-functional or decorative elements in such aspects as balconies and roof canopies. This is partly why Highpoint One and Two seem to sit so comfortably on their sites in contrast to the unrelieved austerity of their Hampstead neighbour Lawn Road Flats.

The received image was one of dazzling whiteness, but colour was very often present. The late arrival of colour reproductions in the architectural magazines meant that a significant ingredient of modern architecture was not recognised by those, and they were the great majority, who drew their knowledge of it from the brilliantly sharp black and white photographs in the influential journals. White always predominated, but the whole range of the Stuttgart Weissenhof estate, in which many of the European masters of the 20s participated, used colour; the Villa Savoye itself had a dark green lower wall and light red or blue screens on the roof terrace; and both the Yorke houses shown here were pink washed, with the projections at Shangri-La in pale blue.

But inside, the archetypal modern house had no room for the arbitrariness of individual tastes. Clutter-free, it left nothing to the fun of chance. The men who shaped it were as determined to follow through the logic of new materials as to reject the old complacent and monstrously unfair world which had finally gone bankrupt in the First World War. They went for a new start, and as

11 F.R.S. Yorke. Torilla, Nast Hyde, Hatfield.
Plans, elevations & axonometric. Pen (485 × 515)

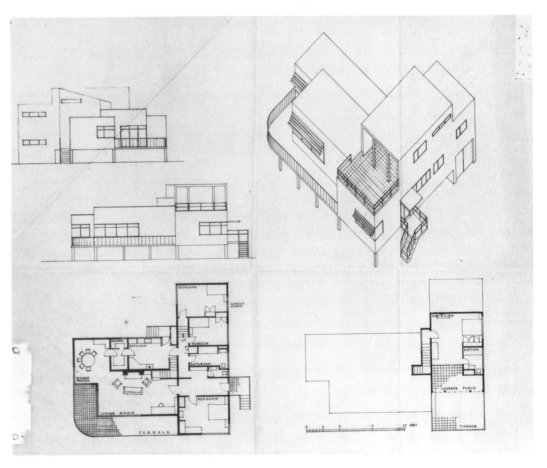

they did so they cleared away the domestic jetsam which the tide of history had so randomly brought to shore. The process seemed to dictate (unhappy word) a whole style of life. But in creating it they underestimated the resilience of the ordinary man, and they were forced into compromise in the end.

The modernists slipped readily, though not always consciously, from the idea of building homes and workplaces to the idea of redesigning society itself. Wells Coates in *Unit One* (1934) asserts that 'as creative architects we are concerned with a future which must be *planned*'. The next year Chermayeff writes (*Architects' Journal* 21 March 1935): 'Architects can no longer concern themselves with construction in a separated professional compartment. They must participate in the reconstruction of society.' And Coates again (*Architectural Association Journal* April 1938): 'As architects of a new order, we should be concerned with an architectural solution of social and economic problems'. This repeated call injected a new moral and political note into architecture (and created a new load of problems for its practitioners).

Over the decade the orthodoxies of the modern house showed a gradual relaxation towards accommodating the diverse needs of its occupants, an increasing realisation of the limits as well as the possibilities of concrete, steel and glass, and an adaptation to the English climate. Two centuries earlier English architects had been so dazzled by Palladio's Villa Rotonda, with its central core for coolness and its porticoed projections on all four sides to provide shade and to circulate the Mediterranean air, that some of them transplanted it without modification to the English countryside. But English climatic needs were entirely different from those of the Veneto. The wits were quick to seize on this. Pope wrote of the 'imitating fools' who 'shall call the winds through long arcades to roar, Proud to catch cold at a Venetian door', and his friend John Gay:

> Doors, windows are condemned by passing fools,
> Who know not that they damn Palladio's rules.

The archetype of the modern house was not so obviously unsuited to the English climate, but it was not after all shaped for our damp and uncertain weather. Fuel and maintenance costs were very high, and a sun terrace is not really a *sine qua non* in Essex.

In his *Modern Houses in Britain 1919-1939* (1977), Jeremy Gould has compiled a gazetteer of 'modern' (i.e. flat-roofed) houses. He lists over 900; less than 100 are north of Cambridge. The southern nature of modern architecture was noted by W.H. Auden in his *Letter to Lord Byron* (1937).

> We're entering now the Eotechnic phase
>   Thanks to the Grid and all those new alloys;
> That is, at least, what Lewis Mumford says.
>   A world of Aertex underwear for boys,
>   Huge plate-glass windows, walls absorbing noise,
> Where the smoke nuisance is utterly abated
> And all the furniture is chromium-plated.
>
> Well, you might think so if you went to Surrey
>   And stayed for week-ends with the well-to-do,
> Your car too fast, too personal your worry
>   To look too closely at the wheeling view.
>   But in the north it simply isn't true.
> To those who live in Warrington or Wigan,
> It's not a white lie, it's a whacking big 'un.

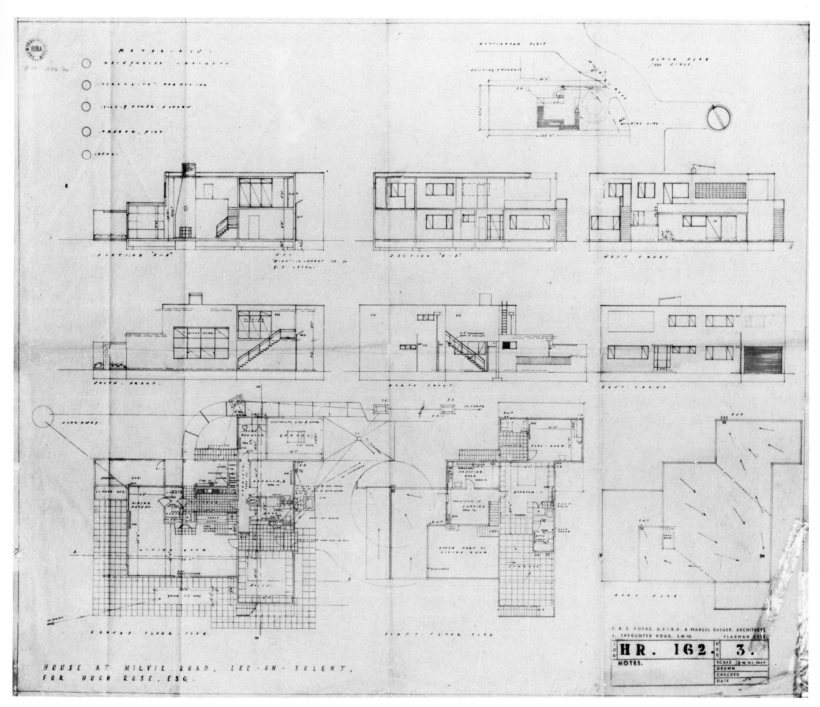

12 F.R.S. Yorke & Marcel Breuer. Shangri-La,
Lee-on-Solent. Plans, elevations and sections.
Pen (625 × 760)

13 Yorke & Breuer. Shangri-La. Garden front

14 Marshall Sisson. 31, Madingley Road, Cambridge

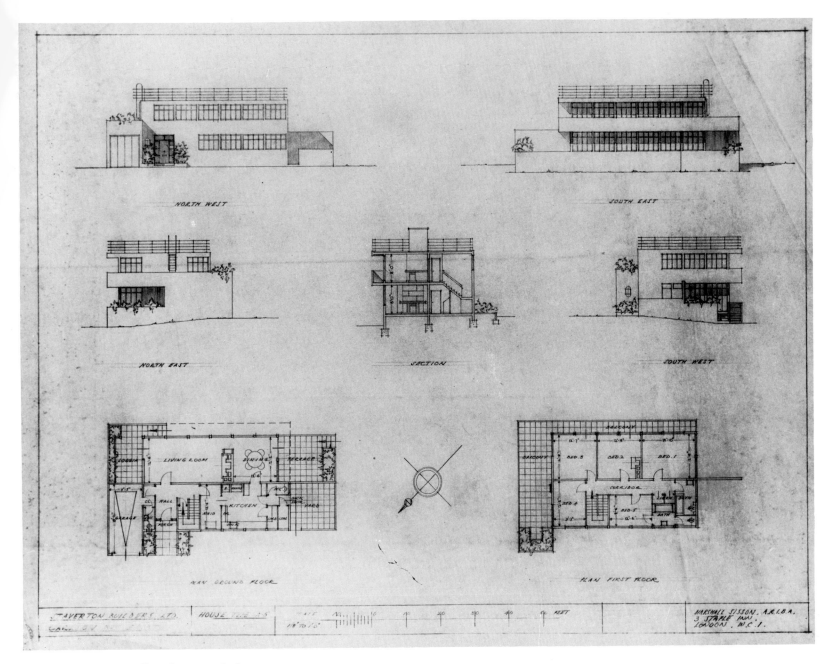

NORTH WEST

SOUTH EAST

NORTH EAST

SECTION

SOUTH WEST

PLAN GROUND FLOOR

PLAN FIRST FLOOR

15 Marshall Sisson. Gull Rock House, Carlyon
Bay, Cornwall. Plans, elevations & sections.
Pencil (585 × 750)

In the 30s the intellectual was expected to take contemporary architecture into his view far more than his successors in our own age. Auden did not in fact care for it. In 1929, caught up by the new spirit, he had called for 'new styles of architecture, a change of heart', but he was to drop this much-used rallying cry from his collected poems on the ground that 'I have never liked modern architecture...and one must be honest even about one's prejudices.'

An early and surprising adherent of modernism was Marshall Sisson (1897-1978), surprising because of his later and greater reputation as a scholarly Neo-Georgian. His 31, Madingley Road, Cambridge (fig. 14) was a substantial brick house, built in 1931 for the don A.W. Lawrence (brother of Lawrence of Arabia). After winning the RIBA's Jarvis scholarship to Rome in 1924, as Basil Ward was to do soon after, Sisson worked for a year in the office of the New York architect John Russell Pope before starting practice in England. In 1933 he built, in Gull Rock House, Carlyon Bay, in Cornwall (fig. 15), a concrete house which took full advantage of its fine site. It was designed to give the widest views over the bay, and on the seaward side both ground and first floor are overhung for protection from noonday sun and Atlantic storm. But by mid-decade Sisson had fallen out of sympathy with the modern movement, in part perhaps because he was so very different in tastes, in temperament, and in political outlook, from its committed advocates.

In 1933, the German emigré Eric Mendelsohn (1887-1953) had arrived in England, to be taken into partnership by Serge Chermayeff (b.1900), and they built their first house at Shrubs Wood, Newland Park, Chalfont St Giles, for R.L. Nimmo. Built in concrete on a terrace with a curving end, the house is perhaps a little less dashing in realisation than Mendelsohn's Expressionist design (fig. 16) suggests.

As Mendelsohn had joined Chermayeff, so Walter Gropius (1883-1969), who had been Director of the Bauhaus at Weimar and Dessau from 1919 to 1928, joined Maxwell Fry when he left Germany in 1934. Fry (b. 1899) was a dominant figure in English modern architecture. Liverpool trained, he had started his career with Neo-Georgian and gentle vernacular buildings, but he was always casting round for the architecture which would express an industrialised society. His membership of the Design and Industries Association, founded in 1915 in emulation of the Deutscher Werkbund, had opened his eyes to the work of Gropius, and the European magazines had shown him what was being done by Taut and Poelzig and Mies van der Rohe. 'Suddenly I saw this comprehensive new architecture accepting the full range of possibilities open to it, the answer to years of doubt and hesitation' (*RIBA Journal* December 1979), and he turned his back 'on the whole medley of styles and mannerisms'. Unlike his fellow moderns, he kept all channels open, through the DIA, through his founder-membership of the MARS Group, and through his active participation in a wide range of RIBA affairs, where he was a Council member from 1933 to 1937. His lively sense of pleasure in architecture formed an ideal counterbalance to the solemn commitment of Gropius in their partnership, though they worked together only between 1934 and 1936, when Gropius left for America.

Their best known work was the Impington Village College, a community cultural centre in the Cambridgeshire countryside, completed long after Gropius had gone to Harvard. But alongside, and contemporary with, Mendelsohn and Chermayeff's Cohen House in Old Church Street, Chelsea (1935-6), they designed at No.66 a house (fig. 17) for the playwright Benn Levy and his actress wife Constance Cummings. Both houses were in rendered brick on a steel frame; unlike its neighbour the Levy house was at right angles to the road. It has now been weatherproofed in hanging tiles, whilst the Mendelsohn house next door has acquired a glass conservatory on the street frontage.

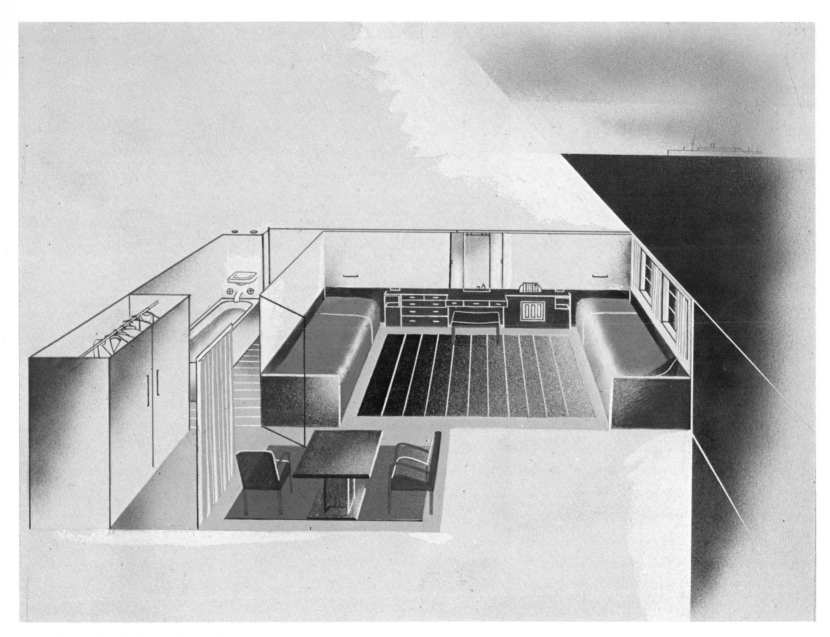

Plate 3: Brian O'Rorke. Decoration for Brochure,
RMS Orion. Drawn by Ceri Richards? Exploded
axonometric. Pen & gouache (245 × 345)

Plate 4: Anne Acland. Coronation decorations,
Bond Street 1937. Perspective. Pen &
watercolour (1015 × 695)

NORTHFIELD

DIAGRAMATIC SECTION OF TYPICAL FLATS

Plate 5: Tecton. Highpoint One (Northfield).
Exploded axonometric. Pencil, watercolour &
gouache (685 × 1020)

Plate 6: Marshall & Tweedy. Viceroy Court,
London NW1. Perspective. Pencil & watercolour
(580 × 1040)

16 Mendelsohn & Chermayeff. Shrubs Wood, Chalfont St Giles. Perspective. Print of original drawing (585 × 785)

17 Fry & Gropius. 66 Old Church Street, Chelsea

18 Fry. Miramonte, Coombe, near Kingston-on-Thames

In 1936-7 Fry designed Miramonte at Coombe, near Kingston-on-Thames, (fig. 18) for Gerry Greene, successively bookmaker, furrier, off-licensee and real estate wizard. Two storeys, in concrete, with a partly sheltered sunroof above, and a long white wall romantically leading away from the house on a paved garden terrace, it is strongly influenced by the Tugendhat house by Mies at Brno in Czechoslovakia, 1930, which Fry himself called 'magical'. The set of working drawings for Miramonte in the BAL would not reproduce rewardingly here, but among them is a delightful sketch (fig. 19) for the house's swimming pool.

19 Fry. Miramonte. Swimming pool. Perspective.
Pencil & crayon (560 × 730)

Obstacle Course

The protagonist of the modern faced far greater obstacles than does his successor today. Out-of-date building regulations, making no allowance for modern techniques, made for out-of-date building methods, and, as Lubetkin pointed out in 1937 (*American Architect & Architecture* February pp.29-30), the effect carried over into the industry itself. Manufacturers knew by heart the old ways and were unwilling to experiment, and foremen, aware of the enormous safety margins prescribed by the regulations, 'do not insist on careful workmanship (this particularly in the case of reinforced concrete), with the result that the general standard of execution and finish has now become very low'.

20

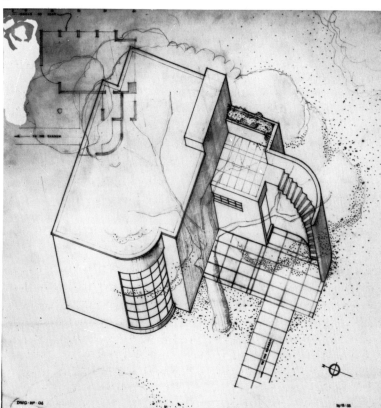

21

22

20 Christopher Nicholson. Kit's Close, Fawley Green, near Henley on Thames

21 Christopher Nicholson. Studio for Augustus John, Fryern Court, Fordingbridge. Preliminary design. Axonometric. Pen & pencil (535 × 520)

22 Nicholson. Studio for Augustus John

The toughest obstacle of all, though, was planning consent. The law insisted that all designs were approved by the local authority, and the committees before which they went largely comprised local businessmen, unlikely to be sympathetic to innovation. Spec building escaped unscathed, but modern designs were vigorously probed, often by panels of architects appointed by the council. Older local architects were thus sitting in judgement on the work of their younger colleagues and rivals, and this could only deepen the rift between the modernists fighting for their ideals amid an almost unshiftable mass, as they felt, of complacent myopics. Few modern practices did not bear the scars of such battles. One skirmish was over Kit's Close, 1936-7, at Fawley Green near Henley-on-Thames for Dr Warren Crowe by Christopher Nicholson. This Mendelsohnian house (fig. 20), which included accommodation for two servants and a chauffeur/valet, was put to an architectural panel by the local authority. Rejected at first, it was finally given approval subject to the insertion of a *cordon sanitaire* in the form of a line of trees to be planted between the village and the house.

Just about this time C.H. Reilly, Head of the Liverpool School of Architecture, returning from the appeal over Chermayeff's house at Bentley Wood near Halland in Sussex (now listed), was to summarise the local council's line of thought in *Building* (April 1937, p.136). 'Bungalows we have heard of, suburban villas we know and indeed have passed by the hundred, but what is this? Something foreign and therefore unpleasant in spite of its whiteness. Indeed one may be pretty sure of that. Our surveyor, that excellent authority on drains and road surfaces, says the building is un-English. What more do you want?' So the blind lead the blind and 'naturally they lead to the nearest ditch.'

Christopher Nicholson (1905-1948) was the younger son of the painter Sir William Nicholson and brother of Ben. Before setting up in practice in 1932 he worked in the office of Val Myer, at a time when Broadcasting House was that office's major job; and he did work too for Jack Pritchard's Isokon firm. In 1935-6 he designed notable buildings for the Dunstable Gliding Club, and twelve years later he was himself killed in a gliding accident. In 1933-4 he built a studio for Augustus John in the grounds of his Fryern Court at Fordingbridge, just as Clough Williams-Ellis was to do a year or so later when he designed the top floor of The Chantry at Portmeirion as a self-contained studio for John. Nicholson's preliminary design (fig. 21) shows a tall studio with a curved glass corner to an otherwise blank south wall and a curved outside stair leading to a small roof terrace. In the final design (fig. 22), built to a precise mathematical grid, the reinforced concrete frame has been raised for maximum light on stilts, in the approved Corbusian manner, though this area has since been infilled to provide an entrance hall and three ground floor bedrooms.

A storm blew up in Hampstead in 1937 with the design for 1-3 Willow Road by Ernö Goldfinger. Born in Budapest in 1902 and educated at the Ecole des Beaux Arts in Paris, Goldfinger practised in Paris for ten years before settling in England in 1934. He was one of the distinguished emigrés who gave assurance to modern architecture in England and one of the few to remain in Britain throughout his working life. By the time he came to design Willow Road it no longer seemed mandatory to think in terms of white cubes (which Goldfinger hated anyway) and he designed a discreetly scaled concrete frame with brick facings and an entirely flexible plan apart from the staircase/plumbing core (figs 23 & 24). 'I really tried', he wrote in the *Architects' Journal*, 11 March 1970, 'to build a late Georgian or Regency terrace in a modern way.' But the Hampstead Heath and Old Hampstead Protection Society was up in arms at the idea. Henry Brooke, its Hon Secretary (and later Minister of Housing) wrote broadsides to the press – '...disastrously out of

23 Ernö Goldfinger. 1-3 Willow Road,
Hampstead. Street frontage

24 Goldfinger. Willow Road. Interior
Perspective of No. 3. Pencil & crayon (330 × 495)

keeping... damage irretrievably the "atmosphere"...' Julian Huxley predictably rallied to the
defence: 'Let the Society protest against the ravages of sham Tudor... but let them refrain from
hindering the development of a true 20th century British style.' A brisk correspondence ensued.
Goldfinger had given the block framed-out windows at first floor level, which ran right across the
facade and effectively offset the height of what was a three-storey group. This particularly irked
Brooke: 'The first floor façade is to be almost entirely of glass, so that the tenants may have a good
look out over the Heath.' In 1970 the building was listed.

Two years earlier Sir Reginald Blomfield (1856-1942) and other Hampstead architects were
attacking a projected house by Connell, Ward and Lucas at 66 Frognal, which would 'upset the
whole character of the neighbourhood'. Connell tartly replied that 'it makes a pathetic picture, this
backwater of architects seeking a refuge with their eyes shut, clutching at a straw which is rapidly
becoming waterlogged'. His bitterness is understandable when we find, for instance, Sir Robert
Tasker MP, denouncing 66 Frognal (the house was ultimately built) as 'one of the greatest acts of
vandalism ever perpetrated in London' (quoted by Basil Ward in D. Sharp, *ed.*: *Planning and
Architecture*, p.83). Willow Road and Frognal between them certainly correct the easily held view
that in some way 30s Hampstead was completely in the hands of the avant-garde, progressive in
the arts and left-wing in politics.

Traditional versus Modern

Blomfield and Connell had already clashed, in a broadcast debate (*Listener*, 28 November, 1934): 'For and Against Modern Architecture' – though the prepositions might well have been reversed since Blomfield was allotted twice the time of his opponent. He preferred to speak of 'Modernismus' so as to stress its alien Teutonic character. 'It has spread like a plague to this country...whether it is communism or not, modernismus is a vicious movement which threatens the literature and art which is our last refuge from a world that is becoming more and more mechanised every day.' This revealing passage at one and the same time suggests xenophobia, an apparent hatred of mechanisation *per se* (though ironically it was Blomfield who had designed the electricity grid pylon) and his view of literature and art as a refuge from the real world.

Blomfield made his position perfectly clear. In the previous year he had written (*Listener*, 26 July 1933): 'As an Englishman and proud of his country I despise and detest cosmopolitanism.' In a phrase he had used before, 'I am', he said to Connell, 'for the hill on which I was born' – to which Connell impudently quoted, 'Home-keeping youth hath ever homely wit'. And already in 1932 he had published *Modernismus*, a wide-ranging assault by a cultivated (and Francophile) scholar deeply dismayed at the threat posed to his whole world since 'the cataclysm of the war has thrown everything into the melting pot'. It was plainly written out of moral duty, a sense that a Gadarene society must be called back from the cliff edge to the broad pastures of Edwardian empire.

Blomfield did not help his argument when he allowed a bilious jingoism to surface. But this must have struck a chord with those who had been in the trenches (or at least on the home front) only a dozen years before. The arrival of the refugee architects which began in the following year, their reputation and the homage paid to them by the modernists, could have done nothing to allay the older generation's feelings of beleaguered insularity. So, in December 1936, Oliver Bernard writes in *Building* (p.520): 'As an Englishman I detest the German invasion of architecture and other things, which is now taking place in my native land.'

The fully rounded reactionary objected as fiercely to the upstart English modernists as he did to the aliens. W. Naseby Adams, a Liverpudlian pupil of C.H.Reilly, who had worked in Lutyens's office, moved after the First World War to London, a world, says his obituarist, Professor Budden (*Liverpool Post*, 24 July 1957), which he was 'apt to regard as one of emasculated gentility' where 'his independent temperament and robust, unpredictable humour may have cost him some clients'. In July 1937 (*Building*, p.310), his choler mixing his metaphors for him, he writes of the ugly and unpleasant architecture which is choking our English garden, produced 'by all the weedy growths which have been allowed to flourish. "Smart Alecs" hold the ribbons. Sensitive gentlemen are temporarily asphyxiated, and it is the sensitive gentlemen who alone can produce architecture; others just build.'

An ingenious theme which Connell brings out in his debate is that 'modern architecture is in the highest sense traditional' because 'from its understanding of the spirit of the past it is able to create, not superficial imitations in this or that style, but living successors in the true line of descent'. Le Corbusier had taken the same position about the principles of Greek architecture. This bold stealing of the enemy's arguments became commonplace. The true traditionalist is not the man who dons a ruff or a full-bottomed wig; he is the man who captures the spirit of his own age. So Yorke and Penn wrote (*op. cit.*, p.108): 'To build in accordance with tradition is not to imitate in one period the obsolete work of a former time. It is to do as the architects of those periods did: to build for contemporary needs, getting the best out of the materials to hand. It is traditional to look forward, not to look back.'

The argument was widely employed. At the RIBA in 1938 a group of younger members led by H. T. Cadbury-Brown and Ralph Tubbs organised an exhibition for the layman on 'The Small House'. Its catalogue makes the same point. 'To clothe and restrict our work by a formula devised by our ancestors for their ends and means is not good manners. It is deceit. Our manners can best be expressed by carrying on the spirit of constant experiment. This is the living tradition inherited by us through many generations'. Blomfield's view was of course the exact opposite: 'A traditionalist, as I understand him, is the only reasonable modernist.'

When in 1932 the Crown Commissioners put forward their proposals to demolish Nash's magnificent Carlton House Terrace, it was Blomfield who prepared a monumental Portland stone replacement, and one group, at 4 Carlton Gardens, was actually built. Opposition was mobilised over a fairly wide spectrum, not least by the *Architectural Review*, that proponent of modernism, and by the MARS (Modern Architectural Research) Group. Out of this campaign was born the conservationist Georgian Group, founded by Robert Byron and the Earl of Rosse in 1937. This was the year Byron published, both in the *Architectural Review* and as a separate pamphlet, *How we celebrate the Coronation*, a ferocious onslaught on the wholesale destruction of classical London taking place at the time of the Coronation festivities. However good the cause, its rhetoric now seems overcharged. Byron, no leftist, invites the reader to 'deluge contempt upon the only nation in Europe that destroys its birthrights for the sake of a dividend' and upon 'the long-nosed vampires of high finance', for today 'architecture, as controlled by speculators and officials, is a forgotten art'. This assertion might have puzzled those great speculators the Adam brothers and John Nash, whose work Byron was so fiercely defending.

Plate 4 shows a different way of celebrating the Coronation, in Anne Acland's prize-winning design for the decoration of Bond Street. Slim white hangings run the length of the street, embellished by crowns at the foot. The end posts, the only part of the scheme not executed, were jutted barber's poles with the royal coat of arms at the base and five crown-like horizontal platforms with concealed lighting spaced up the taper of the posts.

A striking example of an unashamed modern house placed in the great English landscape tradition is St. Ann's Hill Chertsey, 1936-37, by Raymond McGrath, built for the landscape architect Christopher Tunnard, with whom McGrath planned the whole ensemble. Set in 25 acres of 18th century parkland, with the old stable retained as a service courtyard, McGrath's house (fig. 25) gazes down the hill and across the swimming pool, itself shaped to follow the curve of a mature rhododendron clump. To the left can be seen the 1792 Temple of Friendship, and running out towards it from the terrace of the house is a long spur of garden, paved at first, with exotics at the far end, and flanked by a glazed plantroom giving direct access to the house. A wistaria vine has been preserved on the terrace and trained over the glazed opening. The house itself, reinforced concrete with the patterned texture of the wood shuttering kept, is planned as two-thirds of a circle (with all internal fitments and furniture consequently curved), completed by the garden front main living room (fig. 26) with master bedroom over. The house in its setting is a practical demonstration of the true 'living tradition' insisted on by Connell and his modernist colleagues.

It was not only the traditionalists whom the progressives saw as their enemy. They strongly resented too the imitators and vulgarizers, 'people who have no understanding of modern architecture, but who could not have come into being without it'. So J. M. Richards, Assistant

Plate 7: Edward Maufe. Guildford Cathedral. Perspective by R. Myerscough-Walker.
Pencil, watercolour & gouache (550 × 475)

Plate 8: Vincent Harris. Sheffield City Hall.
Perspective with inset plan by H. Charlton
Bradshaw. Pencil & watercolour (495 × 905)

25 Raymond McGrath. St Ann's Hill, Chertsey

26 McGrath. St Ann's Hill. Axonometric. Pen, with pencil inscriptions (530 × 610)

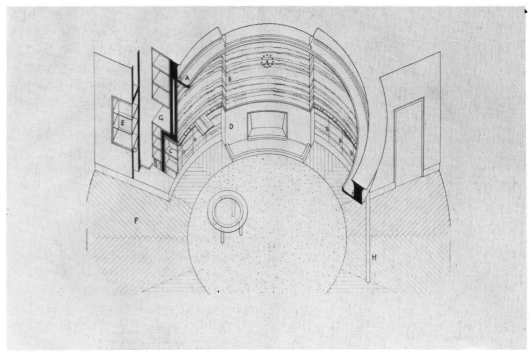

Editor of the *Architectural Review* in his best-selling Pelican book *An Introduction to Modern Architecture* (1940). True modern architecture 'is not, for one thing, a fashionable style of jazz ornament: it is not the custom of building in concrete, or with flat roofs and horizontal window-panes; it is not "functionalism". It is, quite simply, like all good architecture, the honest product of science and art. It aims at once more relating methods of building as closely as possible to real needs.'

As early as 1932 the engineer Owen Williams had denounced 'Façadism' in the *Architectural Review* (November): 'Faking of balance sheets to look right is no better or worse than faking materials to look otherwise – both forgeries'. Nonetheless, after half a century the 'Façadism', the Odeons, the dashing concoctions of Oliver Hill, stand, regardless of any severe consideration of intrinsic merit, with Wells Coates's and Tecton's buildings as valid evocations of the age. But the modernists hated seeing their visual vocabulary stolen.

The trouble was that it was so attractive. In any art, when a particular form reaches a certain degree of appeal, its surface manner starts to seem not only desirable but inevitable, and crowds of lesser figures adopt it. So in the 18th century Pope's poetry achieved a form so masterly that 'every warbler had his tune by heart'. Similarly in the 30s there were many able architects who knew a good thing when they (literally) saw it, and who used the visual elements of modernism as they pleased but without commitment to, or mastery of, the doctrine itself. In and out of the style they ranged, copying away. They were gesturing, sometimes with great elegance, where the form givers were preaching. And few of them would have had the grace to say, as Dryden did about his rewriting of Shakespeare for a more polite age, 'We who ape his sounding words have nothing of his thought but are all outside; there is not so much as a dwarf within our giant's clothes'.

Oliver Hill

A man who slipped in and out of modernism was Oliver Hill (1887-1962). He was so deeply involved in many aspects of the 30s, as his files and scrapbooks testify, that he deserves discussion in some detail here. Educated at Uppingham, where his contemporaries included E. B. Musman and William Pratt (later to change his name to Boris Karloff), he had just started in practice when the First World War broke out. He emerged from it as a Major with the Military Cross to establish a fashionable and hectic practice.

Romantic, enthusiastic to the point of extravagance and sometimes beyond, he moved easily from style to style: Tudor, Georgian, Lutyensesque, Pseudish (in Osbert Lancaster's categorisation) even the Provençal, and not least a Moderne-inflected modernism. But he was more than literally style-ish; there was an aplomb, a dashing elegance running through all his work.

He once wrote tellingly, 'Grace, it seems to me, is the supreme desirability in fine architecture' (*Architectural Design & Construction*, Sept. 1931, p.461). Grace is a word not widely used in the credo of 20th century architects, but it has a rightness for Hill's work. He made the remark the year after visiting the Stockholm Exhibition of 1930 which had opened the eyes of a whole generation to the lightness and freedom made possible by the new architecture. He had also been profoundly interested by the 1925 Paris Art Deco Exhibition, as his library, left to the BAL, shows. It must have been here that his taste for glass and chromium, onyx and alabaster, for the whole new game of High Chic, was quickened. He was to put a stamp of exotic luxury on all his modern buildings but with a sensitivity carrying them clear of the merely flashy or tawdry.

The persuasiveness of his modern essays presented some problem to the committed. They knew he was not one of them, but some of them recognised his *sui generis* quality and found him a rather uneasy place in their expositions of modernism. Thus Raymond McGrath in his *Twentieth Century Houses* (1934) pays him a finely impenetrable compliment. Not one of his houses 'is like another or true in feeling to any but the present time and that only in the widest sense of the word' (p.102).

McGrath's yes-but-no tribute appears in his appreciation of Joldwynds, Holmbury St. Mary, Surrey, 1930-33 (figs 27 & 28). In 1925 Hill had already adorned Holmbury with Woodhouse Copse, a highly picturesque thatched and timbered house making much use of existing Tudor materials. Its new neighbour was utterly different, a superbly sited group of white shapes, with semi-circular staircase window, topped by a white drum, and displaying Hill's liking for softening rectangularity with a curved wing. Each suite of rooms had its own sun terrace.

His client was the barrister Wilfred Greene, later Lord Greene, Master of the Rolls and an honorary Fellow of the RIBA. Hill had done work both for Greene – a remodelled Kentish

27 Oliver Hill. Joldwynds, Holmbury St Mary. Preliminary perspective. Pencil, crayon & chalk (330 × 680)

28 Hill. Joldwynds

farmhouse near Sandhurst – and for Mrs Greene – a conversion in Bryanston Square – but he rapidly ran into trouble at Joldwynds. Greene displayed an icy coldness on finding that 'the skylight above my lavatory was broken and a large piece of tar fell onto the lavatory seat where it still remains'; and his tone sharpened over the smuts which showered from the oil heating and the fumes which made it impossible to venture in to see what was wrong.

His wife's criticism of the furniture pulls no punches. After commenting on 'the absurdly expensive floor' she continues, 'It may interest you to know the merits and demerits of the furniture which you designed for us', (and which can be seen in figure 29). 'It is *all* too *high*, and too heavy and cumbersome. The big settee is too long...It is hard as iron and your suggestion of cushions is not practical as the back is so upright that there is no room for them. I notice that you sat on my best and softest cushion in order to be comfortable...Carnera's chair is so called because only Carnera [the heavyweight boxer] could possibly be comfortable in it...I shall move it to an unused room...The coiffeuse is too heavy to wheel – hence the wheels are useless...' and so relentlessly on. 'You may be glad of these practical details the next time you are designing furniture. It would all photograph nicely... Unfortunately Joldwynds was meant for a house to live in, not a lovely film set'.

A letter to Hill from Christopher Spenser, a house guest at Joldwynds, comments, 'May I say how much my wife and I admire your arrangement of the rooms?' and adds, making it likely that his letter postdates Mrs Greene's, just quoted, 'They do not, I fear, look either so artistic or so pretty now'. Another undated letter, this time from Marion Dorn the textile designer, says that she and McKnight Kauffer think Joldwynds 'absolutely grand'. The client wants her to go down there: 'I would like to make a rug for that house more than anything I know of,' and indeed she did.

29 Hill. Joldwynds. The living room, from *Country Life*, 15 September 1934, p.280

30 Oliver Hill. Holthanger, Wentworth

Hill did all he could to counter criticisms and make good the shortcomings, but the house continued to give structural trouble, and in June 1936, with Hill's consent, Greene called in Lubetkin of Tecton to supervise new cement rendering of the external brick walls. Lubetkin finally advised Greene that a new and smaller house could be built for the cost of full restoration of Joldwynds, and in 1939 he completed a four bedroom house with a pitched roof in the grounds of Joldwynds.

Hill's Holthanger, at Wentworth in Surrey, 1933-6 (fig. 30), for Miss Newton, has many similarities with Joldwynds. Again on a fine site and in brick rendered white, it has a glazed staircase tower rising the height of the building and a blue-tinted cylindrical water tower as a roof feature. The large sitting-room has at its west end a glazed screen which opens out into a semi-circular sun-room, as can be seen on the plan (fig. 31), which also shows Hill's liking for long shallow curves.

Hill moved easily in fashionable society. His clients ranged from Syrie Maugham (with Sybil Colefax one of the two leading society interior decorators), whose Villa Elisa at Le Touquet he worked on, to aristocratic patrons like Lord Vernon and Lady Forres, for whom he built classical town houses in Chelsea Square, and Lord O'Neill, for whom he designed the huge Palladian mansion of Shane's Castle in Co.Antrim, which was overtaken by the war and not executed. Between 1933 and 1937 he designed Holthanger in the International Style, a number of strictly Neo-Georgian town houses, the Morecambe Hotel (plate 23), the housing estate at Frinton (figs 113 & 114), the modern Prospect Inn at Minster-in-Thanet (fig. 106), and the British Pavilion at the 1937 Paris Exhibition (plate 20), as well as much furniture design and exhibition work.

His chameleon-like talents can be seen in his design (fig. 32) for a house in the Highlands, exhibited at the Royal Academy in 1936 but not executed. This substantial house, as so often in his work in a magnificent (though unidentified) setting, has gabled dormers in a slate roof, and balconied venetian windows in the projecting pavilions at either end of the garden front.

31 Hill. Holthanger. Ground plan, not as executed (550 × 805)

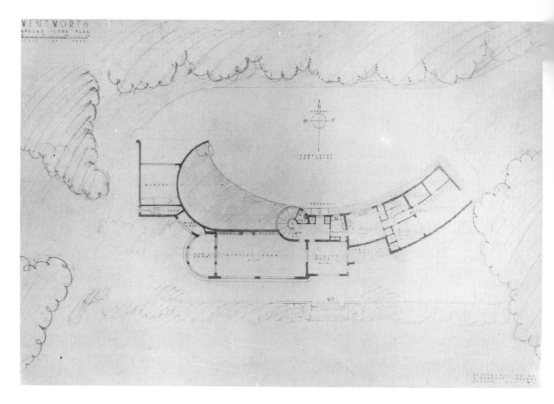

32 Oliver Hill. Design for a house in the Highlands. Perspective by J.D.M. Harvey. Pencil, charcoal & watercolour (340 × 555)

The Modern Flat: Wells Coates and Jack Pritchard

In the 20s the concept of the minimum dwelling had been central to the ideas of Le Corbusier. J.J.P. Oud in Holland and Gropius at the Bauhaus were much occupied too with the idea, and in 1927 all three of them, together with Peter Behrens, Bruno Taut, Mies van der Rohe and other major European figures, demonstrated at the Weissenhof housing exhibition in Stuttgart the current ideas on rationalisation, standardisation and minimal housing. Two years later the second of the Congrès Internationaux d'Architecture Moderne (CIAM) produced an influential report: *Die Wohnung für das Existenzminimum* (Minimum Income Dwellings). This was designed to establish the workers' needs and how to meet them, though its conclusions, it might uncharitably be thought, did not necessarily accord with what the workers actually wanted. Ernst May, the Frankfurt City Architect, where the Congress had been held (and who himself had contributed a design to the Weissenhof), advanced some chilling notions about people's having the right only to a 'ration dwelling' calculated according to their biological and sociological needs.

At much the same time Wells Coates in England was developing similar ideas about minimum space requirements. Coates (1895-1958) was born in Tokyo of Canadian parents. He took an engineering degree at the University of British Columbia and wrote a Ph.D dissertation at London on 'The Gases of the Diesel Engine'; and he thought of himself, as his letterhead (fig. 91) shows, as an architect-engineer. In 1924 he joined the office of Adams and Thompson, where he worked with the young Maxwell Fry, and his first independent work was the design of shops in London, Bournemouth and Brighton for Cresta Silks.

The concept of the old, settled, permanent home was becoming outmoded, he said in 1933. 'We don't want to spend as much as we used to on our homes. So the first thing is that our dwellings have got to be much smaller.' His own restless exploratory nature gave particular force to his view that 'we cannot burden ourselves with permanent tangible possessions, as well as with our real new possessions of freedom, travel, new experience – in short, what we call "life" ' (*Listener* 24 May 1933, p.819).

A paradox which was to drive right through progressive thought can already be seen. Smaller homes, more economically planned, more cheaply built, yes. But what would the unemployed coalminer or shipworker have thought when he heard Coates's broadcast identifying modern life with freedom, travel, new experience? The advanced English architect, despite his political and social leanings, rarely came face to face, at least in his professional life, with the real working class.

Coates held consistently to this position. Five years later, he wrote, 'We move after work, easily, at least within national frontiers; we move for holidays across frontiers; we move away from the old home and family; we get rid of our belongings, and make for a new, an exciting freedom' (*Architectural Association Journal*, April 1938, p.449). His attitude was widely shared. Another characteristic expression of it came from Maxwell Fry in 1934: 'The programme of house living has changed, the structure is changing, even the family unit is breaking up and re-joining in new formation, as witness the idea of hotel and hostel living and the new emergence of the one-room flat' (John Gloag, *ed.: Design in Modern Life*, p.36).

Through the decade Coates worked at his deeply held concern. Simple social justice meant a decent home for everyone; and this was feasible only with mass production and standardisation. For the mass-produced house 'you would plan a large number of standard units capable of assembly in a large variety of forms and finishes and colours. And you would assume (you would

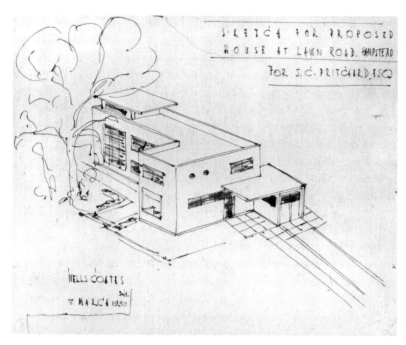

33 Wells Coates. House at Lawn Road,
Hampstead. Unexecuted. Perspective. Pen &
wash (210 × 250)

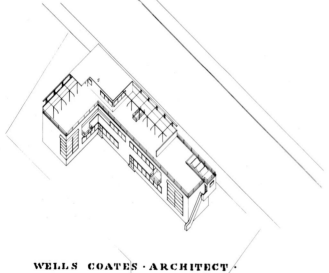

34 Wells Coates. Pair of linked houses, Lawn
Road, Hampstead. Unexecuted. Isometric. Pen
(340 × 495)

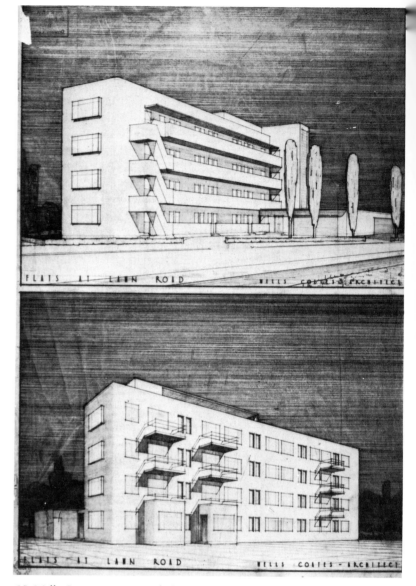

35 Wells Coates. Lawn Road Flats, Hampstead.
Perspective. Pencil (685 × 510)

have to) that your mass-produced methods would be matched by mass-planning methods in siting the new dwellings in new group formations, bearing some ordered relation to your work, your play, your entertainment, and to the systems of communication which link these into a community' (*Architectural Association Journal*, April, 1938 p.447). Hence his interior layout designs, his built-in furniture and his standardised Sunspan houses.

In 1929 an event of the first importance to him took place when he met Jack and Molly Pritchard. Pritchard had joined the Estonia-based Venesta Plywood Company in 1925 and had become familiar with Le Corbusier's work when working in Paris in 1929. The following year, encouraged by John Gloag, prolific writer on design and architecture, who worked for the advertising agency holding the Venesta account, he got Le Corbusier to design the Venesta stand at the Olympia Building Trades Exhibition. The Pritchards found that they shared many of Coates's views, and they were hungry for first-hand experience of modern European architecture. In 1930 they visited the Weissenhof together, and in 1931 they went with Chermayeff to Germany, visiting the Bauhaus in Dessau and meeting Mendelsohn in Berlin.

On a site they had acquired in Lawn Road, Hampstead in 1930, the Pritchards invited Coates to design a house for them (fig. 33). This quickly developed into a pair of linked houses designed as a single unit (fig. 34), and over the next two years, as the Pritchards' ideas for a 'minimal housing' block of flats took shape, Coates produced a number of variants on the unit plan. By now the client was Isokon ('Isometric Unit Construction'), a firm set up by the Pritchards in 1931 to produce houses, flats and furniture on unit principles with Coates as their designer. In the 1933 Exhibition of British Industrial Art at the Dorland Hall in London Isokon displayed a minimum ('Isotype') flat by Coates, an ingenious one-room home for those who travelled light, full of sliding doors, fitted cupboards and furniture which folded away. The exhibit was intended to attract deposits from potential tenants for the block of minimal flats now projected for Lawn Road, but leaping costs and trouble with the planning authority put a stop to the plan to use strict Isotype principles throughout.

The outcome was Lawn Road Flats, opened in 1934, a four storey block of 29 flats, of which 22 were 'minimal'. Figure 35 shows the developed form of the block, built in concrete with the outside walls left as they came from the shuttering and simply painted cream, and, on the road side, a stark horizontal stress given by the open cantilevered galleries widening at one end into a diagonal fire escape. Visual pleasure for the casual passer-by took no high place in the design. In a manuscript obituary (1958) of Wells Coates, later printed in the *RIBA Journal*, Raymond McGrath describes the flats as 'an essay in the economy of space' and adds that Coates's work 'had often a sort of puritan logic about it which did nothing to ingratiate it to the public'. These were homes for the young, mobile middle classes, mostly intellectuals, and a natural base for the refugee artists and architects coming in from Nazi Germany, several of whom Pritchard employed as designers for Isokon furniture.

In the year Lawn Road Flats opened Isokon planned another development, (fig. 36) at St Leonard's Hill, overlooking Windsor Great Park, on the site of a derelict Thomas Sandby house of the 1770s. Royal permission was granted and much to Wells Coates's anger Gropius and Fry were commissioned. 69 flats, restaurant, ballroom, Turkish bath, tennis and squash courts, swimming pool, even skittle alley, were to be set in 33 magnificently landscaped acres. The appeal of the publicity brochure was aimed less at the Hampstead intellectual community than at those who would find Eton 2 miles, Ascot 8, useful assets. 'They have been designed for those who care for the country, whose manner of living is intelligent, and whose social standards are high...busy

36 Fry & Gropius. Flats at St Leonard's Hill, Windsor. Unexecuted. Perspective. Pen, pencil & wash (495 × 965)

people, tired of expensive and crowded living in the small fashionable centres of the West End...' A page from the brochure (fig. 37) shows different flat layouts and their rentals, with or without maid or hotel services.

In a letter of 23 March 1970 Maxwell Fry comments: 'The scheme was nearly all Gropius, but I did a series of drawings contrasting our development that preserved landscape with the devastation normal to spec. building development.' Sadly it proved impossible to raise the capital needed, the more so since Pritchard fell ill, and the scheme was abandoned.

Meanwhile Coates was working out his ideas for unit housing, in his Isotype dwellings and in the Sunspan house, initially for Isokon but transferred by him, misguidedly, to a conventional builder with whom he soon fell out. This standardised house type was planned along a diagonal north-south axis for maximum sunlight. Between 1934 and 1938 at least fourteen Sunspan houses were built, mainly single-storey but a few two-storey and one of three storeys. Within their symmetry all have in common a remarkably free plan, allowing the shape and size of rooms to be altered at will, and all retaining a south-facing living room and bedroom. Figure 38 shows one of the first to be built, for Mrs H.M. Hill at a cost of £1,250. It is a bungalow at Welwyn, (1934-5) now drastically altered, with Sunspan's characteristic curved and glazed southern aspect. Another, of 1936 for A.G. Whale, planned for a site at Cranleigh, is very similar to the two-storey version of Sunspan, the prototype for which had been shown by Coates at the 1934 *Daily Mail* Ideal Home Exhibition. Coates's sketches (fig. 39) employ two different modes for working up presentation perspectives for his client; but there is no record that the house was built.

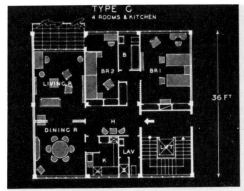

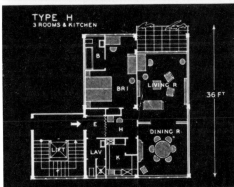

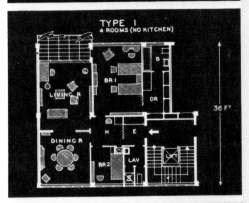

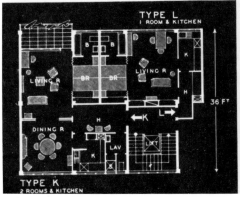

FIVE SPECIMEN FLATS

TYPE G 4 ROOMS AND KITCHEN

LIVING ROOM 12'6" × 16'0"	BEDROOM 1 12'6" × 16'6"
DINING ROOM 12'6" × 12'6"	BEDROOM 2 8'0" × 15'6"

TYPE H 3 ROOMS AND KITCHEN

LIVING ROOM 12'6" × 16'6"	BEDROOM 12'6" × 16'6"
DINING ROOM 12'6" × 12'6"	

TYPE I 4 ROOMS (NO KITCHEN)

LIVING ROOM 12'6" × 16'0"	BEDROOM 1 16'6" × 12'0"
DINING ROOM 12'6" × 12'6"	BEDROOM 2 8'0" × 9'0"
	DRESSING ROOM

TYPE K 2 ROOMS AND KITCHEN

LIVING ROOM 12'6" × 16'0"	BED RECESS 6'6" × 10'0"
DINING ROOM 12'6" × 12'6"	

TYPE L 1 ROOM AND KITCHEN

LIVING ROOM 12'6" × 16'6"	BED RECESS 6'6" × 10'0"

TYPE	INCLUSIVE RENTS	WITH HOUSEMAID SERVICE	WITH HOTEL SERVICE
G	£315–370	£355–410	£375–430
H	£220–255	£250–290	£265–300
I	£235–270	£265–300	£280–320
K	£175–195	£200–220	£210–230
L	£125–145	£140–160	£150–170

Every flat has a hall, kitchen and bathroom, in addition to the number of rooms quoted, except type I which has no kitchen. A limited number of type I flats will be let furnished with full hotel service from 10 to 12½ guineas per week.

The development of St. Leonard's Hill, Windsor, has been promoted by the Isokon Control Company, Ltd., the proprietory company of the Lawn Road Flats, Hampstead, N.W.3, from whom further particulars can be obtained. *Telephone:* Primrose 6054.

Or from, Messrs. Hampton & Sons, Ltd., 20 St. James' Square, London, S.W.1. (Telephone, Whitehall 6767) and in Hampstead and Wimbledon.

38

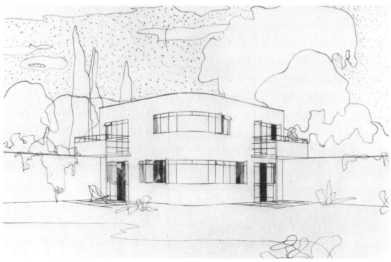

39a

39b

38 (*Facing page*) Wells Coates. Sunspan bungalow, Welwyn

39a & 39b (*Facing page*) Wells Coates. Sunspan house, Cranleigh. Unexecuted. Perspectives. Pen (420 × 545); pencil & crayon (370 × 505)

40 Tecton. Highpoint One, Highgate

The Modern Flat: Tecton and others

As Lawn Road Flats were reaching their final form, their Highgate neighbour Highpoint One was being designed by Lubetkin and Tecton. Born in Tiflis in 1901, Berthold Lubetkin had trained in Russia and Berlin, moving to Warsaw, then Paris in the mid 20s, where he studied, like Goldfinger, in the atelier of the reinforced concrete master Auguste Perret. He supervised the construction of Melnikov's remarkable Soviet Pavilion at the 1925 Paris Exposition and set up in practice with Jean Ginsberg. His conviction of the need for a socialist society might have sent him back to Russia had not Stalin's glacial hand already begun to freeze the innovatory fervour of Soviet architecture, and in 1930 he came to England to practise in partnership with Tecton, a group of young AA graduates – Anthony Chitty, Lindsay Drake, Michael Dugdale, Valentine Harding, Godfrey Samuel and R.T.F. Skinner.

Highpoint One, 1935, was their first major housing job. The moving spirit behind the clients, Northfield Property Company, was Gestetner, the 'neocyclostyle' tycoon. Lubetkin had met him through Warburg the banker, whom he had known in Paris, and Gestetner mentioned that a project of his for housing Gestetner employees in a North London block of flats had fallen through since the site had been snapped up by another promoter. If Lubetkin himself could find a site, he would back Tecton for a commercial block. Acting on shrewd advice, Lubetkin chose his district, had a drink in a promising public house, and asked the publican if he knew of any possible site. 'Exactly opposite – across the road', said the landlord of the first pub he visited, in Highgate; and Highpoint One was born (fig. 40).

Designed on a Cross of Lorraine plan with one flat per storey in each of the four arms, two in the central spine, and one at each end, it was an eight-storey reinforced concrete structure containing 60 flats in all. Raised on Corbusian stilts, the whole ground floor became a free open space; above, all was cellular. Except for the overlooking inseparable from a right-angled plan, complete privacy was achieved, with no partition walls between neighbours except in the central spine. Rents ranged from £130 to £234 a year, including hot water and central heating, compared with £96 a year for the cheapest Lawn Road Flats. Highpoint was an exercise in community living, but with its service flats and its maids' bedrooms (16 of them), it was community living for the comfortably off, and a block planned for a social mix was in the event colonised by middle-class intellectuals.

Plate 5 is a diagrammatic section of the flats. This unusual form of presentation contrives at once to show external treatment, constructional details and the handling of spaces within the flats. At the bottom left is one of Highpoint's distinctive cantilevered balconies. Lubetkin had already used this arabesque ('cyma') shape in the balconies of a small terraced group of houses he had designed with Pilichowski at Plumstead in 1934; and the motif added an inviting friendliness to the otherwise severe exterior of Highpoint. The block received an accolade when Le Corbusier himself wrote of it in the *Architectural Review* (January 1936) as 'the seed of the vertical garden city...an achievement of the first rank...For a long time I have dreamed of executing dwellings in such conditions for the good of humanity.'

Highpoint Two followed on the adjoining site in 1936-8. By this time local residents had formed a Highgate Preservation Society to prevent such palpable vandalism occurring again, and Lubetkin had to expend much energetic ingenuity in getting planning approval. 'The Charme of Ye Old Village' (fig. 41a) unflatteringly depicts Highgate Village. The main purpose of the drawing, however, was to show, alongside Highpoint One, unrelated to it and cutting off light and view, the

41a Tecton. Highpoint Two, Highgate. Aerial perspective. Print with grey wash added (635 × 950)

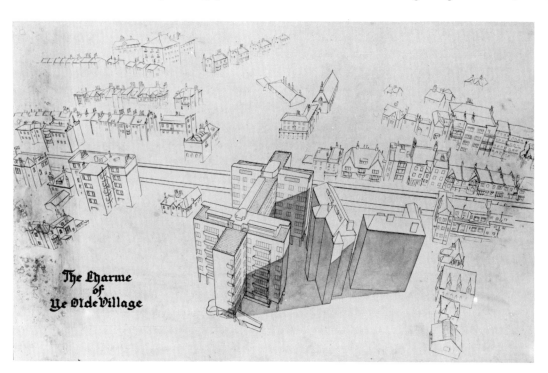

54

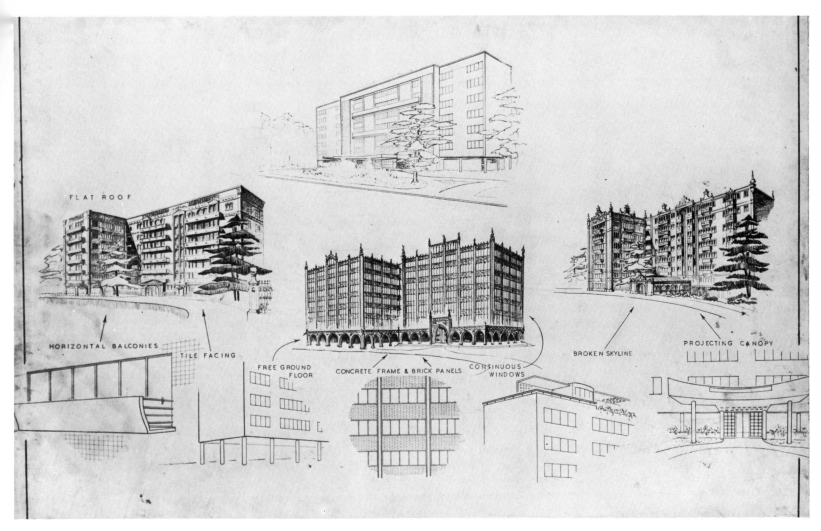

Labels on image: FLAT ROOF · HORIZONTAL BALCONIES · TILE FACING · FREE GROUND FLOOR · CONCRETE FRAME & BRICK PANELS · CONTINUOUS WINDOWS · BROKEN SKYLINE · PROJECTING CANOPY

41b Tecton. Highpoint Two, Highgate.
Perspectives & details. Print with grey wash
added (635 × 950)

outline of a newly proposed block to which the Council had given provisional approval. To
prevent this destruction of Highpoint's amenities Gestetner bought the site. Now that, under the
Town and Country Planning Act, the Council were able to exercise aesthetic control, Tecton
advanced for their verdict alternative treatments before submitting final designs. Figure 41b shows
how this was done. Each of the elevations contained tongue-in-cheek historical allusions, and each
incorporated elements of the design Tecton wanted to put forward. Once the Council's view of
each had been established the scheme as built was submitted and approved (fig. 42a).

Aimed at wealthier tenants than its predecessor, it was aligned in site with Highpoint One, but its
plan was rectangular and its materials richer, glazed tiles, glass blocks on the staircase towers and
marble in the hall. Lubetkin intended it as a challenge to the severity of Functionalism; it was time
to move on. His solution attracted the ire not only of the Preservation Society but equally of the
austerer modernists. Especially provoking was the use of two casts of caryatids from the
Erechtheion to support the entrance canopy (fig. 42b). These could be interpreted in various ways.
They constituted a surrealist juxtaposition; they could be counted on to shock opponents of
Highpoint One; they were an ironic assertion of age-old continuity, and a visible expression of the

modern architect's claim to be the true inheritor of tradition; they were also beautiful. The *Architectural Review* (October 1938), straight-faced, advanced the view that Tecton had adopted the standard classical solution in the absence of a true modern equivalent, which would be substituted when in due course it had been created. This was not taken seriously.

Another mid-30s block was Pullman Court at Streatham Hill (1934-5) by Frederick Gibberd (b.1908), who had been assistant to Berry Webber before setting up his own practice in 1932. Designed as three predominantly rectangular blocks of varying heights grouped round treed courts, it comprised 218 one, two and three-room flats with roof-gardens. Construction was mostly concrete, and the walls were painted brown, pink, grey and blue. The drawing illustrated

42a Tecton. Highpoint Two. The garden front

42b Tecton. Highpoint Two. The entrance canopy

Plate 9: Berry Webber. Hammersmith Town
Hall. Perspective by Cyril Farey. Pencil &
watercolour (550 × 660)

Plate 10: Oliver Hill. Methley School, Yorks.
Aerial Persepctive by J.D.M. Harvey. Pencil with
crayon & watercolour (515 × 710)

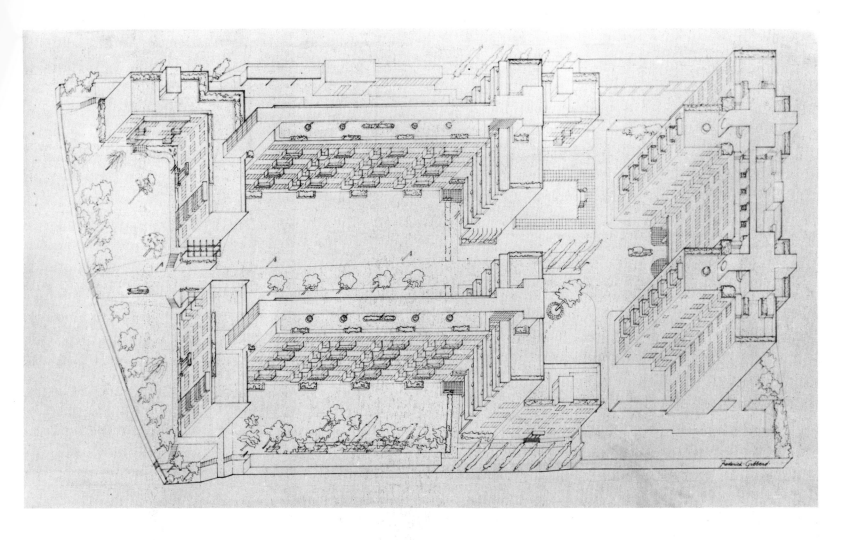

43 Frederick Gibberd. Pullman Court,
Streatham Hill, London. Axonometric by Robert
Townsend. Pencil (490 × 845)

(fig. 43) was by Robert Townsend, General Secretary of the MARS Group in 1934.

Viceroy Court, Prince Albert Road, NW1 (1936) by C. Beresford Marshall (1899-1944) and W. Tweedy (plate 6) was a luxury block, brick-faced on a reinforced concrete frame, on the north west side of Regents Park. Far less committedly modern than Highpoint or Lawn Road Flats, it is a kind of muted resumé of modern motifs – the inset balconies, the glazed and rounded corners (except on the end wings at the rear where the balconies are semi-circular instead) and the horizontal accent of the railed roof gardens. In that sense up to date, it nonetheless did not adminster the shock treatment of the real modernist building. It skilfully exploits the interplay of solids, voids and shadows, and has an unassuming character which does no violence to the noble buildings of a century earlier that border the Park.

44 J.H. Forshaw & C.G. Kemp. Pithead baths and recreation centre, Betteshanger Colliery, Kent, 1934

Working Class Housing

We have already seen that many modern architects had as their ideal the rebuilding of society itself: but the reality was a humbling restriction to private houses, mostly for wealthy intellectual sympathisers. For the client of these idealists was not a world waiting to be born but the well-to-do private citizen in search of a home (with adequate provision for the servants). During his stay in England Gropius built only two houses; both were for socialists, 66 Old Church Street, Chelsea for Benn Levy (fig. 17) and at Shipbourne in Kent for Jack Donaldson, more recently Lord Donaldson, Labour Minister for the Arts.

Nor were the blocks of flats done by the moderns, however strong their aspirations, generally for the workers themselves. The working-class was being housed by the public authorities, whose work at the time was professionally held in low esteem. There was a famous row in 1938 when the seigneurial Goodhart-Rendel, President of the RIBA, referred in passing to public architecture as 'stale chocolate'. Bureaucratic impediments, interference from the Borough Engineer, and a built-in discouragement of individual initiative in the public office, all added to the feeling that the state-salaried architect was professionally second-class. It was lack of opportunity elsewhere as much as social idealism which was the spur for public recruitment.

But there were exceptions. Forshaw & Kemp's Dudokian pit-head baths (fig. 44) and recreation centres for the Miners' Welfare Commission helped to solve the problem of retaining personal enthusiasm in a substantial public office by each project being carried through from start to finish

45 Lancelot Keay. St Andrew's Gardens, Liverpool

46 Herbert J. Rowse. Camden Street, Birkenhead

47 Maxwell Fry, Robert Atkinson, Grey Wornum & C.H. James. Kensal House, Ladbroke Grove, London

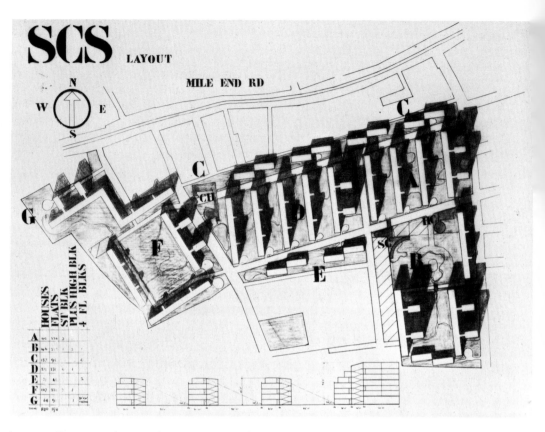

48 Wells Coates. Slum clearance scheme, Mile End Road, Bethnal Green, London. Unexecuted. Layout plan. Pen, pencil & crayon (585 × 760)

by a small team under a senior assistant. And slum clearance at its best produced, in Liverpool under Keay and Leeds under Livett, high density flats for low income tenants with a range of communal services on the pattern of the Karl-Marx-Hof in Vienna.

Lancelot Keay (1883-1974), Director of Housing and later City Architect of Liverpool, was formally responsible for the erection of 35,000 flats and houses. St. Andrew's Gardens,1934 (fig. 45) were designed without reference to the bleak tradition of working class housing. The blocks comprised 316 flats, with pitched roofs but with a firm horizontal emphasis provided by the laterally patterned brickwork, the generous windows and the balconies. Very similar was the 1935 scheme for Camden Street, Birkenhead (fig. 46) by Herbert J. Rowse (1887-1963). As well as a good deal of housing, Rowse, who had trained under Reilly, designed the Liverpool Philharmonic Society's concert hall and the entrances and ventilation stations for the Mersey Tunnel (now listed). Like St Andrew's Gardens, Camden Street displayed the humane approach created under the aegis of Keay: again the facades relieved by the simplest means, alternate banded courses of slightly projecting brick, vertical patterned brickwork below the cornice and tall curved entrance arch.

In 1936 the Gas Light & Coke Company invited Robert Atkinson (1883-1953) to form a committee for the design of Kensal House in Ladbroke Grove, and he got Maxwell Fry, Grey Wornum, and C.H. James, with Elizabeth Denby as housing consultant, to join him. Fry, who had already designed another group of working class housing with Elizabeth Denby at Sassoon House in Peckham, was responsible for executing the plan, which included a nursery school, clubrooms and workrooms. Built on the site of a gasholder, the gentle curve of the flats (fig. 47) faced morning sun on the bedroom side and afternoon sun on the living room side, whilst on the opposite side of the curve, utilising the shape of the original gasholder, stood the nursery school, with its playground in the space between. Each flat had two balconies, one of them recessed for drying clothes.

In 1938-9 Wells Coates was to complete a luxury block at Palace Gate, Kensington, for his client Randal Bell, but for some years he and Bell had already been pursuing ideas, and a site, for working class housing. At the New Houses for Old Exhibition at Olympia in 1934 the MARS Group had presented an analysis of the problems (though deliberately holding back from design solutions) associated with Bethnal Green housing. Coates had been prominent in this work, and he and Bell continued to search for a site where the private developer could build a rehousing scheme which would yield an economic return. In the Beaumont Estate in the Mile End Road they found a bathroom-less slum group of 750 houses. Coates set to work in 1937 to design a layout (fig. 48) which would rehouse twice as many families in modern conditions on the same site with no increase in rent. But the war put a stop to the scheme's implementation.

Churches

The 30s saw a number of churches built, notably in the expanding suburbs. Along with a good deal of suburban housing, and the Park Royal Underground Station of 1935-6, the partnership of Welch, Cachemaille-Day and Lander designed some idiosyncratic and powerful examples, among them St Saviour at Eltham in south east London, 1932-3 (fig. 49). This was a lofty brick structure, flat-roofed and lit by five tall narrow pairs of blue glass windows. The squat tower, as the plan shows (fig. 51), is in fact the roof of the choir. In its strongly North Germanic interior, the dominant brick texturing is relieved at one point only, by the concrete reredos with its Christ figure (fig. 50). St Saviour was awarded the RIBA's London Bronze Medal, and the calibre of the jury of assessors is worth noting. They were Sir Giles Gilbert Scott, Grey Wornum, Edward Maufe, Joseph Emberton, Robert Atkinson, C.H. Reilly, A.B. Knapp-Fisher (President of the Architectural Association) and T. S. Tait of Burnet, Tait and Lorne, who among much other interesting work had designed the pioneer Silver End Village in Essex in 1926-7 to serve workers at Crittall's metal window factory. There were three lay assessors: Valentine Goldsmith of the BBC, Gerald Barry of the *News Chronicle* and Frank Pick of London Transport.

Another church designer, mainly in the north west, was Francis X. Velarde (*c*.1897-1960), a pupil of Reilly's and a Roman Catholic. His St Gabriel Blackburn, 1932-3, (fig. 52b) an Anglican church, has square pew ends, two cylindrical tubs as lectern and pulpit, a startling art deco chromium reredos and light fittings which would not be out of place in a 20s roadhouse (fig. 52a). Less quirky was St Wilfrid's Anglican church in Brighton, 1932-4 (figs 53 & 54) by H.S. Goodhart-Rendel (1887-1959). Goodhart-Rendel was a scholar who had a profound interest in 19th century architecture when such tastes were conventionally thought merely eccentric; his manuscript index of Victorian Church Builders is in the BAL. He was also a musician, a convert to catholicism, the owner of a noble country house at Hatchlands in Surrey (now the property of the National Trust), and had been a Guards officer in the First World War. Indeed, he was the author of the *Grenadier Guards Squad Drill Primer*, an unlikely happening which found some slight echo in the Second World War when the Home Guard manual on camouflage was written by the influential Surrealist painter and writer Roland Penrose. St Wilfrid was a massive structure on a sharply sloping site

49 Welch, Cachemaille-Day & Lander.
St Saviour, Eltham, London

with meticulous brick patterning and an unlit mansard roof in red tiles. Its architect's concern for acoustics led him to use asbestos lining in the roof, and this posed some threat during the scare over asbestos forty years later; but in 1981 the church received Listed Building status, though its future remains precarious.

In 1929 Sir Edwin Lutyens had received the commission for the new Roman Catholic cathedral in Liverpool, but his majestic designs were never to be realised and were abandoned after the Second World War. Altogether less impressive was Maufe's Guildford Cathedral, begun in 1932, of which Myerscough-Walker's bold north elevation (Plate 7) generates an excitement not fulfilled by the building itself. Maufe won the commission in open competition, and among his papers are a number of congratulatory letters. Three, in widely differing manners, are quoted here.

Raymond Unwin, PRIBA, writes, 'I am delighted to think that the new building is in such good and sympathetic hands. When I met your good lady the other day, I said that impartiality', (Unwin was one of the competition assessors) 'did not allow me to give her good wishes for your success; but I can now very heartily give congratulations.'

The next day Clough Williams-Ellis writes briefly and breezily from Portmeirion, 'Hurrah, and bravo! I have only just heard the news, which delights me'.

And on the following day again Voysey, now 75, writes a curiously hedged-about letter: 'Many times I have felt inclined to write and congratulate you and tell you how pleased I was to hear you had won the Guildford Competition, and each time I have checked myself because I thought it was an unkindness to make you feel you had to write in reply. But at last I can write in such a way as to tell you on no account whatever to write any acknowledgement but wait till we meet. I have heard many remarks made by architects all of which without exception were favourable to the award. Indeed many have said what an easy competition to assess, yours being so far ahead of the others... Now please take me at my word – I always mean what I say and I shall not be pleased if you do not acquiesce'.

50 Welch, Cachemaille-Day & Lander.
St Saviour, Eltham. Interior

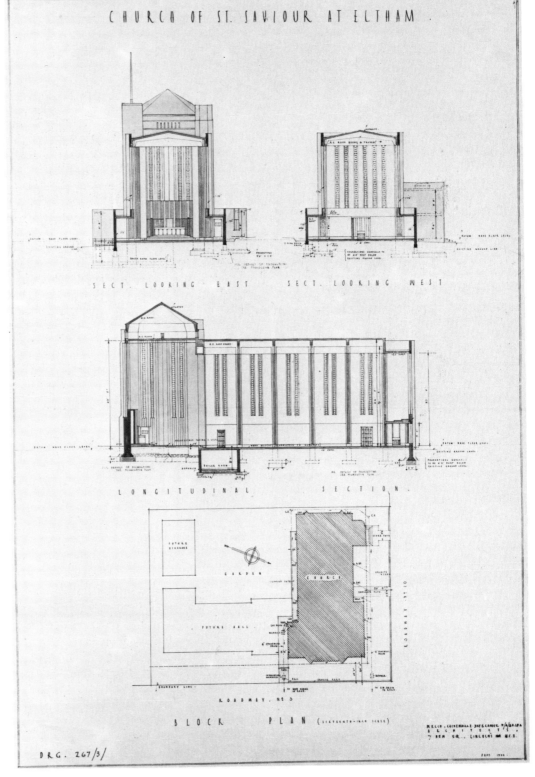

51 Welch, Cachemaille-Day & Lander.
St Saviour, Eltham. Plan & sections. Print with
coloured washes added (980 × 685)

52a Francis X. Velarde. St Gabriel, Blackburn.
Interior

52b Velarde. St Gabriel, Blackburn

53 H.S. Goodhart-Rendel. St Wilfrid, Brighton

54 Goodhart-Rendel. St Wilfrid, Brighton.
Axonometrics. Print (665 × 1020)

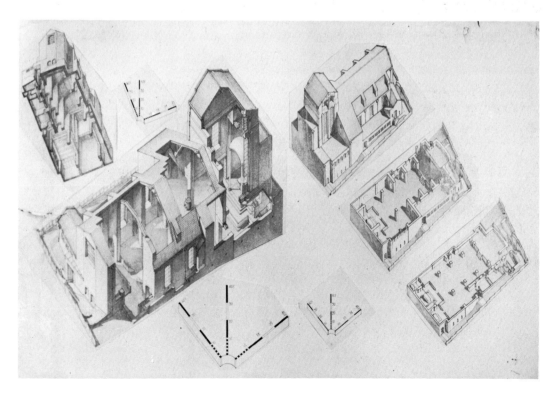

55 Vincent Harris. Sheffield City Hall. Interior

56 Sir Henry Wood. Letter to E.J. Carter, June 1934, concerning the acoustics of Sheffield City Hall

At the present moment I am very concerned with the rebuilding of the concert platform in the City Hall, Sheffield, which was built without consulting a single conductor or experienced musician, & is without doubt the worst orchestral platform in the world. We are hoping to get the "lions" removed for the Sheffield Musical Festival next October, as they completely upset the sitting of the chorus and the orchestra

Civic Buildings

Civic buildings sprouted between the wars, many of them commissions won in competition by solid traditional architects. Chief among these was Vincent Harris (1876-1971), who did municipal work up and down the country, at Sheffield, Manchester, Leeds, Bristol, Kingston-on-Thames, Nottingham and Cardiff. Sheffield City Hall was won in competition in 1920 and completed in 1932, a timescale comfortably outstripped by his block of government offices on the east side of Whitehall. Competition winners in 1914, they were not finally built, basically to the original designs, until the 1950s – by then, some felt, not without a dismaying incongruity. Sheffield City Hall (Plate 8), in white stone, has a portico of Corinthian columns framed within a rectangular front, whilst at the rear is an open semi-circular colonnade. In sharp contrast is the entrance lobby (fig. 55), three domed compartments lavishly decorated with Moorish motifs by George Kruger Gray, whose fame rests mainly on his coinage designs.

The concert hall within aroused dismay among musicians, as is shown by a letter of June 1936 to the Editor of the *RIBA Journal* from Sir Henry Wood, father of the Promenade Concerts (fig. 56). Wood's indignation over the acoustics incidentally highlights the dilemma inherent in running a magazine which tries to be both a lively commentary on the architectural scene and the house journal of the RIBA's corporate members. Carter, the Editor, replied, 'I should very much like to

57 Berry Webber. Peterborough Town Hall. Interior perspective by Cyril Farey. Pencil & watercolour (650 × 795)

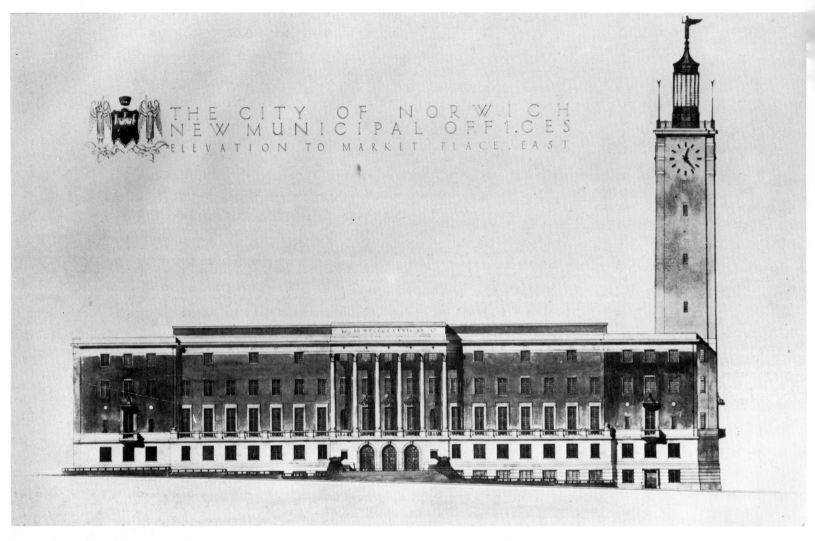

THE CITY OF NORWICH
NEW MUNICIPAL OFFICES
ELEVATION TO MARKET PLACE, EAST

58 C.H. James & S.R. Pierce. Norwich City Hall.
Elevation. Print of original drawing (410 × 610)

publish your letter but unfortunately (sometimes) we have to be desperately careful about publishing remarks which may be interpreted by our members as criticisms of their works. Your downright reference to Sheffield I am afraid would excite more than the passing wrath of the architect.' He proposed an ingenious variation which would allow the informed to take the point without naming names, but by then Wood had moved on to other things and his commination remained unpublished. The 'lions' to which he refers were a prominent pair of substantial stone lions flanking the performers' 'entrance of honour'. They were in fact removed, and stand now at the head office of the Derbyshire Stone Co. in Matlock, the firm which had done the stonework for the building.

Another Town Hall specialist was Berry Webber (1896-1963), who in his early days had worked in Harris' office. In the study for the Staircase Hall at his Peterborough Town Hall, 1931, (fig. 57), drawn by the perspectivist Cyril Farey, only the figures give any clue to the building's date, which could readily have been any time during the century. This design indicates accepted official standards at the time when the competition was under way for the new RIBA building. A later work of Webber's was Hammersmith Town Hall, 1936-9 (Plate 9), again drawn by Farey, a rather dispiriting version of the monumental municipal, with an odd little intrusion of the modern in the external glazed corner stair. The building is now listed.

The successful design for the Norwich City Hall, 1932-8, won in competition by C. H. James and S. R. Pierce (1896-1966), owed its inspiration directly to Sweden and specifically to the much admired Stockholm Town Hall of 1911-23 by Ragnar Ostberg. Pierce's building (fig. 58) had a central colonnaded portico rising the height of the building from the first floor level. The podium was stone-faced, the superstructure brick and the cornice surmounting it stone. His watercolour (fig. 59) shows the City Hall's relation to the church of St Peter Mancroft and to the statue of Sir Thomas Browne which gazes at it across the Market Place.

59 C.H. James & S.R. Pierce. Norwich City Hall. Perspective by S.R. Pierce. Sepia pen & wash (475 × 550)

Broadcasting House

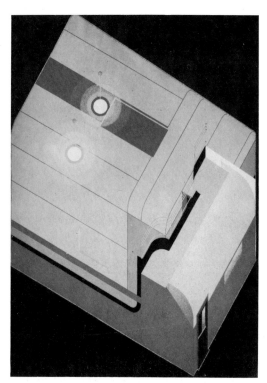

60 Raymond McGrath. Preliminary design for BBC Dance Music and Chamber Music Studio. Axonometric. Gouache (695 × 520)

In 1927 the British Broadcasting Company had become a public Corporation, and the search began for new premises, led by Valentine Goldsmith, Assistant to the Controller and later Director of Business Relations, and Marmaduke Tudsbery Tudsbery, the Corporation's Civil Engineer. The BBC was close to settling on Dorchester House in Park Lane when it learned of another opportunity in Foley House, Portland Place. Lord Foley's original town house had stood on the site of what is now the Langham Hotel, facing north up Portland Place. The site in question, however, was not this but James Wyatt's own smaller house, also confusingly called Foley House, at the south east corner of Portland Place. Wyatt's house had been demolished in 1928 for the development of luxury flats by a financial syndicate whose architect was Val Myer. The site, which the BBC promptly leased, presented some particular problems. The great London sewer, built of brick in 1830, lay under it and had to be enclosed in concrete; and beneath it too was the Bakerloo Tube line, though, startlingly, the engineers were apparently unable to say precisely where. But the problems were overcome, and Myer and Tudsbery successfully completed Broadcasting House in 1932. Predictably the outcome was a compromise between the conflicting needs – to affirm the new technology and to maintain neighbourly relations with the Adam buildings in Portland Place. Reith himself, the BBC's Director General, did not like it, and R.S. Lambert, Editor of the BBC journal *The Listener*, called it 'a Leviathan of a building' in his autobiography; 'not the dove or the eagle but the white elephant should be its crest' (*Ariel and All his Quality*, 1940, p.150). Originally rented – the ground-floor rooms facing Portland Place were designed for shop use – the freehold was purchased by the BBC in 1936, with (among many others) the proviso that certain callings, 'a meat slaughterman', 'a quasi-medical or quasi-surgical establishment' and 'a brothel or bagnio keeper', were not to be pursued on the premises. The covenants, claims Edward Pawley in *BBC Engineering 1922-72* (p.105), have been scrupulously observed to this day.

In November 1929 a Studio Design Committee was set up, and Raymond McGrath, a 26 year old architect with one previous job to his credit, was appointed special consultant. McGrath (1903-1977), an Australian who had won the Sydney University Medal for English Verse, came to England to pursue architectural research at Cambridge in 1926. Three years later he met the Cambridge English don Mansfield Forbes (1889-1936) and was commissioned by him to remodel the interior of his Victorian house Finella. The result had little to do with the modern movement and a great deal to do with the exotic luxuries of Art Deco. There were folding copper doors with black nickel handles, a hall ceiling of ribbed greeen glass, a metal and glass bathroom, and blue, black, silver and gold everywhere. Outside it McGrath placed a concrete totem pole dedicated to Finella, the legendary Scottish queen who built an all-glass palace and plunged to her death in a fathomless waterfall. Forbes was instrumental in forming the first, short-lived modernist group, the Twentieth Century Society, in 1930, and Finella was a meeting place where you might find Chermayeff and Maxwell Fry, Morton Shand and de Cronin Hastings of the *Architectural Review*. Forbes's friend Lance Sieveking took his BBC colleague Valentine Goldsmith (both were later to join the MARS Group) to see the work of the young architect who had transformed the house, and it was this visit which led to the BBC's remarkable patronage of modern architecture over the design of studios.

As colleagues McGrath chose Dorothy Trotter (Talks Studios), Chermayeff, aged 29, (Orchestral and Talks Studios), Wells Coates, aged 34, (Special Effects, News, Gramophone Studios), and, for

61 Raymond McGrath. BBC Vaudeville Studio. Perspective. Crayon (340 × 340)

the Religious Studio, Edward Maufe, aged 46. This relatively youthful team, faced with new and exceedingly difficult technical problems, worked under the tight control of the BBC's engineers. McGrath himself designed the Dance Music and Chamber Music Studio (figure 60 shows a preliminary design) and the Vaudeville Studio (fig. 61). BBC policy was to try to introduce into the sterile setting of the studios a humane environment for the broadcaster. So McGrath's basement Vaudeville Studio was laid out as a miniature theatre with stage, spotlights and audience for the performers, who normally wore full evening dress.

Maufe's Religious Studio was again a small room, given presence by rising through two floors . Maufe provided a suitably ecumenical gravity by simple abstract fittings under a pale blue decorated ceiling. The choice of decoration, however, offered difficulties. The signs of the zodiac and other generally aspiring symbols were felt perhaps to offend religious susceptibilities. These were followed by symbols of the Four Evangelists, only in turn to be rejected in favour of a star motif. Figure 62 shows Maufe's design with the ceiling at an interim stage; figure 63 a photograph of the studio as built.

According to *Exchange & Mart* (15 September 1932) 'one or two speakers are so attracted by the appearance and acoustics of this studio that they use it in preference to the other studios. The French lessons, I believe, come from the Religious Studios'. The authority for this improbable belief is unclear, but acoustic treatment was naturally of the very highest importance throughout. At the beginning of the decade Swedish glass, foreign textiles and the like were widely held to be superior to any home products, but the economic crisis of 1931 caused the BBC voluntarily to renounce a sizeable part of its income, and 'the efforts of the decorators employed resulted in persuading' British firms to manufacture to these superior foreign standards (*BBC Yearbook*, 1932, p.77). There is a glimpse, in a letter from McGrath to Maufe, of his stipulating 'the three kinds of building boards of Empire manufacture which are approved from the acoustic point of view', a letter which shows what detailed supervision the young architect in overall charge exercised over a distinguished colleague twenty years his senior.

63 Maufe. BBC Religious Studio

62 Edward Maufe. Preliminary design for BBC Religious Studio. Perspective. Pencil & wash (330 × 245)

Plate 11: Ernö Goldfinger. Design for an
expanding nursery school. Pencil & crayon
(315 × 505)

Plate 12: Gilbert Scott. New Bodleian Library,
Oxford. Perspective by Lesslie K. Watson. Pencil
& watercolour (540 × 760)

Plate 13: Berry Webber. Daniel Neal's store,
Kensington. Elevation by H.L.G. Pilkington.
Pencil & watercolour (650 × 980)

Polyfoto Ltd.
ground floor waiting lounge
looking towards bar & end wall
mirrors.

Plate 14: Raymond McGrath. Design for a
Polyfoto studio. Interior perspective. Pencil &
crayon (280 × 375)

The Architectural Profession

In the 1890s a famous debate had raged on whether architecture was an art or a profession, and of course there are radical differences between architecture and the other arts. An important one has already been plain in our account of the practical problems facing the modernists: the architect must have a client. The poet or the sculptor can work on regardless and disregarded as long as the candle burns and the bread supply holds out. The client does not direct their labours: no-one ever told Eliot that Four Quartets were too many. Again, while words, wood and stone remained the primary tools of the writer's and sculptor's craft, the architect was confronted by materials which had no aesthetic pedigree. Ezra Pound's injunction to 'make it new' had special force for him. But from the client and the planning authority to the building industry and the workmen on site there was opposition to everything untried, in design, materials and method.

The surge of political and social debate brought another difficulty in its train, expressed by the painter William Coldstream in a broadcast talk (*Listener*, 15 September, 1937): 'The slump had made me aware of social problems, and I became convinced that art ought to be directed to a wider public; whereas all ideas that I had learned to regard as artistically revolutionary ran in the opposite direction'. The poster artists, men like McKnight Kauffer and Tom Eckersley, managed to bridge this gap in their work for the great public patrons, such as Shell, London Transport and the Post Office, and so to acclimatise the man in the street to the direction modern art was taking. The need to make a living persuaded other artists willy-nilly to lessen the gap. Paul Nash and Ben Nicholson did posters, Auden and Britten did commentaries and soundtracks for documentary films. But this kind of popularisation was less readily open to the committed architect.

In the 20s architects were entering their profession largely through apprenticeship bolstered by night school, and their first experience beyond junior assistant level was often in interiors and product design work. Emberton, Chermayeff, Wells Coates, McGrath all started, and often continued, in this area. It was a notable period for interior and furniture design, exemplified by the grand rivalries of Syrie Maugham and Sibyl Colefax, and by the fact that even the uncompromising painter Francis Bacon began work as a decorator and rug designer. Le Corbusier, Mies, Gropius, Breuer all practised furniture design as an integral part of their work, the last two for Isokon during their stay in England, and this was equally true of non-modernists like Hill and O'Rorke, both of whom reckoned themselves to design the furniture for the houses of their wealthy clients. There was nothing new in this: it was in the central tradition of architecture. What was new was that it presented opportunities for design which helped to make good the distinctly short supply of private or public building clients.

Still practising in the 30s were men like Sir Ninian Comper the church architect, whose belief in architecture as an art precluded him from joining his professional body. Despite such questioning of the architect's true role, the range of arguments for professional organisation seemed overwhelming, and the RIBA developed drastically between 1919 and 1939. By the later 30s, following a number of Registration Acts, entry to the profession was controlled and the right to use the title 'architect' legally restricted. The first generation of highly trained post-Registration architects was emerging. They brought with them the particular flavour of their Schools, whether it were Liverpool under the galvanic guidance of Sir Charles Reilly or the more modest Hull, whose Head from 1934 to 1939 was Leslie Martin, leading protagonist of modernism and editor, with the sculptor Gabo and the painter Nicholson, of the international constructivist manifesto *Circle* (1937). Under the more traditional regimes, of Richardson and Corfiato for instance at

64 John Betjeman. Letter to E.J. Carter,
March, 1932

THE ARCHITECTURAL REVIEW
9, Queen Anne's Gate, Westminster, S.W.1
PROPRIETORS
THE ARCHITECTURAL PRESS
LIMITED
TELEPHONE VICTORIA 6936

7th March, 1932.

Edward Carter, Esq.,
    Royal Institute of British Architects,
      9 Conduit Street, W.1.

Dear Librarian,

    I told the L.C.C. about Bossom. It is a
brilliant idea. I do not know whether they have
replied.

    Hoping this reaches you as it leaves me,

      Yours till death,

          J. Betjeman.

P.S.   de Cronin Hastings, with characteristic
self-effacement, refuses to go to the
R.I.B.A. dinner, so that I shall be obliged
to go in his stead. Iwould be very much
gratified if youcould pull a string so that
I sat near somebody interesting, instead of
as is usually the case next to   of
THE BUILDER; though a delightful man with a
family at Upminster in Essex, is inclined to
pall after a few hours.

    I should like to have those blocks from
ARCHITECTURE as soon as possible.

STATEMENTS IN THESE LETTERS CANNOT BE GUARANTEED BY THE MEDICAL OFFICERS

London's Bartlett School, the student might not be confronted at every turn by Le Corbusier and Gropius, but he would soon meet them in the pages of the magazines. He might not feel moved to do, or try to do, likewise, but their work stimulated excitement and endless discussion. But as an educated man might enjoy both Swinburne and Eliot, or Bach and Cole Porter, so for the architectural student the world was all before him where to choose, and an admiration for Lutyens did not disqualify him from a very different admiration for Lubetkin, whom he would quickly find in the brilliantly designed *Architectural Review*.

Architectural journalism flourished in the 30s at a level hard to imagine today, and the leader was unquestionably the *Architectural Review*. Extravagant pains were taken, in design, typography, and illustration to produce a handsome object in its own right, and though it moved steadily from a cultivated and rather dilettante eclecticism at the start of the decade towards unremitting advocacy of the modern movement when J. M. Richards and Nikolaus Pevsner started writing for it, it rarely deserted its preferred tone of wit and irony and suave insiderism. Osbert Lancaster, Robert Byron, John Betjeman, Morton Shand were regular contributors, and book reviewers ranged from D. H. Lawrence to Connolly, Evelyn Waugh and Auden (the latter under the *plus ça change* headline 'What is wrong with architecture?'). The high spirits of life at Queen Anne's Gate in the early 30s are engagingly caught in a letter (fig. 64) to E. J. Carter from the young John Betjeman.

The RIBA and its Building

When the 28-year old Carter (1902-1982), from Cambridge and the Architectural Association, joined the RIBA as Librarian and Editor of its *Journal* in 1931, he arranged for Stanley Morison to redesign the *Journal's* typography and for Eric Gill to make a new badge, based on the Lion Gate at Mycenae which had been used as the Institute's badge since its earliest days a century before. The result, shown here in Gill's original signed proof (fig. 65), with its motto in his Perpetua capitals, did not escape its critics, one censorious, and unpublished, correspondent of the *Journal* describing it as 'two monkeys smoking cigarettes'. But its distinction was widely acclaimed, and there was distress when it was abandoned thirty years later, though the BAL retains it for its Library bookplate. The RIBA was controlled, wrote Carter in 1979 (*Architectural Review*, November, p.325), by 'middle-aged, middle-class, widely cultured men – no women – with middle-sized practices... despite their general acceptance of customary forms the leading men were well disposed to allow the RIBA to be a breeeding ground of new ideas, not least to the extent of allowing the RIBA Library freedom to open a window to the thoughts of the whole world.' The freedom allowed to Carter himself, at one and the same time *Journal* editor, controller of a physically and intellectually 'open' library and dedicated advocate of modernism, is witness to this liberal attitude.

In 1934 the RIBA celebrated its hundredth birthday. The Centenary Conference, for which Rex Whistler designed a special card (fig. 66), was held in Grey Wornum's newly opened building in Portland Place. There was an excellent Exhibition of International Architecture, in scope wide enough to embrace both Sir Guy Dawber and Mies van der Rohe (the 154-page catalogue had a cover by John Farleigh: see figure 67). There were receptions and presentations and tributes, and not least there was a Centenary Banquet in the Guildhall.

65 Eric Gill. Engraved design for RIBA Badge: Proof

66

67

Here the toast 'The RIBA' was proposed by the Prince of Wales, and he took the chance to raise a subject much on his mind since his visits to the 'Distressed Areas'. These, he said, had impressed on him the urgent need for slum clearance and rebuilding. In the past architects had concentrated on abstract ideals in satisfying the individual client. Now they must consider 'a greater and far more important ideal – designing and working for the great majority... You are charged with the great and honourable duty of educating the people of your country to better living more than you are charged with idealising units of architecture.' He pleaded for wider streets and higher buildings, with traffic separation, and especially for carrying the 'principle of mass production over into architecture and the building trade' as the only way of raising living standards in an age where life was 'far more collective in principle than individualistic'.

All this was a long way from the benign generalities usually offered on such occasions, and must have created some stir, though perhaps rather less than we might think. Sir Giles Gilbert Scott, the President, had written in his Introduction to the International Architecture exhibition catalogue: 'We cannot continue to tolerate the poverty, ill-health, waste and ugliness of disorder.' And the Prince himself had already started a series of clubs for the unemployed. The second of them, the Feathers Club in Norland Gardens, in London (subscription a penny a week) had opened at the beginning of 1934, designed by Wells Coates and David Pleydell-Bouverie. In May of the previous year *Design for Today* reported the Prince as saying to the Carpenters' Company, 'Never be too proud to copy anything you may see abroad that you think is better than you could have produced at home', an exhortation which must have come as disturbing in a world of 'Britain is Best'.

The lasting achievement of its Centenary Year for the RIBA was its new building in Portland Place. This had been the subject of an open competition in 1930 which had been won by Grey Wornum (1889-1957), seen here on site (fig. 68). There had been 284 entrants, and the assessors were faced with over a mile of drawings. Wornum's winning design (fig. 69) was considerably reduced by RIBA economy cuts in 1932, and it lost its top three storeys (to the pleasure of Goodhart-Rendel who did not care for 'that building's taste in hats' (*Architect & Building News*, 26 June 1932, p. 417)). He had had to design a building worthy of and acceptable to a profession then as now disparate in its tastes. Neither monumental classical nor stripped modern would do. And he had to remember too the 18th century rhythms of Portland Place; his building would have to meet the standards of the Howard de Walden Estate. So a compromise was both inevitable and appropriate.

His building was generally approved. The modernists, naturally enough, disliked it, and at the other extreme Sir Herbert Baker (who did not enter) observed of the entries as a whole that 'there seems to have been a common impulse to give expression to the present-day philosophy which has been so tersely defined by Sir James Barrie: "Whatever was is wrong" ' Philip Tilden took a different line over Wornum's entry: 'it will give the effect to visitors that English architects must be making millions'. But professional responses generally made much use of words like refinement and urbanity, despite Clough Williams-Ellis' judgement that the competition produced 'a tedious mass of uninspired stodge'.

From its great bronze entrance doors to the plaster reliefs on its ceilings, artists, not quite all of the first rank, used a plethora of motifs to symbolise architecture. In the main reception hall, for instance, the piers were decorated by Bainbridge Copnall with 'Man and his Buildings through the Ages'; figure 70 portrays Wornum, with monocle – he had lost an eye in the war – talking to Maurice Webb, Chairman of the Building Committee, while behind them sits Ragnar Ostberg,

66 (*Facing page*) Rex Whistler. Invitation card for RIBA Centenary Conference 1934. Pen & wash (235 × 165)

67 (*Facing page*) John Farleigh. Cover for RIBA Catalogue 1934

architect of the Stockholm Town Hall. Appropriately so, for Ostberg's building, seen in relief behind Wornum's elbow on the pier, had done something to influence his design though a more direct source was another Stockholm building, the City Library by Asplund. Several other artists exercised their talents about the building, not least the architect's wife Miriam, who was responsible for all the fabrics and colour schemes. She is depicted at least twice among the decorations, and her initials are slyly inscribed on the floor of the entrance. Most of the glass work was done by Jan Juta. It was Raymond McGrath, however, who incised the 'Six Ages of Architecture' on the windows outside the Council Chamber. Figure 71 shows the first three installed. The corridor-free building and its ingenious but never oppressive decoration speak worthily for the Neo-Swedish taste of its time. It was listed in 1970.

68 Grey Wornum, architect of the RIBA building, on site

69 Grey Wornum. The RIBA building, Portland Place, London. Perspective by J.D.M. Harvey. Pencil & crayon (625 × 580)

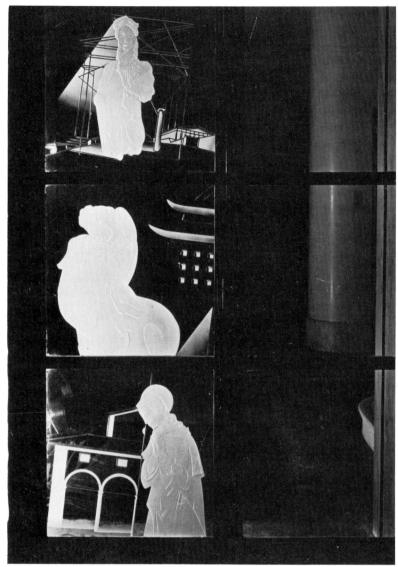

70 Grey Wornum. The RIBA building. Interior
of Florence Hall.

71 Raymond McGrath. RIBA building:
incised glass windows

72 E.B. Musman. Peckham Health Centre, London. Unexecuted. Perspective. Pen & watercolour (405 × 620)

Health Centres

A striking aspect of 30s social idealism is shown in the concept of the Peckham Pioneer Health Centre. Health was not just a matter of freedom from the doctor's surgery and the hospital; it was altogether more positive. The Centre was to be a place where whole families could find relief from the devitalising pressures of urban living, and come together for relaxation, social pleasure, and regular preventative overhauls. For the organisers it presented an ideal, humane setting for developing constructive, in distinction to merely curative, policies of social medicine. The idea of community care, of a centre where all (for payment of a very modest subscription) might seek pleasure, exercise, and dedicated help over their problems, was a fine example of the brave 30s belief in the possibility of a better future for ordinary people.

The moving spirits at Peckham were a husband and wife team of doctors, Scott Williamson and Innes Pearse. After a modest start in a private house in 1926, they commissioned E.B. Musman (1888-1972) to design a major Pioneer Centre at Peckham in 1930, which would include swimming bath, gymnasium, cafeteria and reading room. His design (fig. 72) was exhibited at the Royal Academy that year, but the doctors' ideas were not fully worked out, nor was adequate finance available. There was probably some element of incompatibility between client and architect, and his rather stiff proposal, where only the size of the figures in the perspective jolts one into realising the modest scale of his building, came to nothing.

Three years later all was ready. As intending clients the doctors wrote a highly unorthodox letter to a selected group of architects, asking for assurances that the Centre could be built for £25,000, seeking firm opinions on the minimum cost and on the sum for which it could certainly be built, and calling for replies by the end of the week. The sketch plans they provided were the work of J. M. Richards, who had set out in graphic form the doctors' ideas about spaces and their relationships as a guide to the architect when the time came to appoint one.

73 Owen Williams. Peckham Health Centre,
London. Perspective. Pencil & wash (530 × 750)

Papers in the BAL show that the doctors' approach caused a fair number of raised eyebrows. One of the eminent figures approached reported the matter privately to the RIBA as 'a pretty bad example of the kind of thing we are out to stop', adding that the realisation of 'the enthusiastic doctor's sketch plans' would not be 'a great plum for anybody who is not a genius in cajoling cranks'. What looked like developing into a serious row about professional ethics was forestalled when the clients settled for the brilliant Sir Owen Williams (1890-1969), who as an engineer was not subject to the RIBA code of practice.

Before the First World War Williams had been Chief Aircraft Designer for Wells Aviation. As a civil engineer he introduced into Britain structural methods pioneered on the continent of Europe, notably by the Swiss engineer Maillart; and during the 30s he designed the Boots Factory at Nottingham, the Daily Express building (with Ellis & Clarke) and the Empire Pool at Wembley. The Peckham Pioneer Health Centre (1934) is seen here (fig. 73) in the original design perspective, which seems to suggest a pastoral setting, though in fact it was opposite Sassoon House flats of the same date by Maxwell Fry and Elizabeth Denby. It was a reinforced concrete structure grouped round a central swimming pool. Its open grid of concrete stanchions allowed flexibility in using the internal spaces. The gymnasium is on the left, the theatre on the right, and between them is the children's covered playground with glazing which slides away to make it an open air space. Above the playground are the shallow bowed fronts of the main social gathering place.

Tecton's Finsbury Health Centre of 1938 (figs 74 & 75) was no visionary social and preventative centre like Peckham. But an earlier unexecuted scheme for a tuberculosis sanatorium had already started Lubetkin thinking about social medicine. The interior of the Finsbury Centre, with mural by Gordon Cullen, was adorned with didactic slogans – 'Fresh Air Night and Day', 'Live Out of Doors As Much As You Can' – and signs beckoning to mysteries like Solaria. But its function was simply to gather into a hospitable whole the scattered health services, dental, maternity, child welfare, tuberculosis, of the Borough. It was laid out on a slightly splayed H-plan with a wedge-shaped block bisecting the cross-bar. Constructed of concrete and glass bricks, it was faced with glazed and easily cleaned tiles. At Finsbury Tecton continued their move away from functional purism, already signalled at Highpoint Two. The entrance face is inclined forward, and the blank ends of the wings are clad with twelve large faience tiles with diamond decorations to mark the point where each touches its neighbour.

74 Tecton. Finsbury Health Centre, London.
Exploded axonometrics. Pen & wash (950 × 1160)

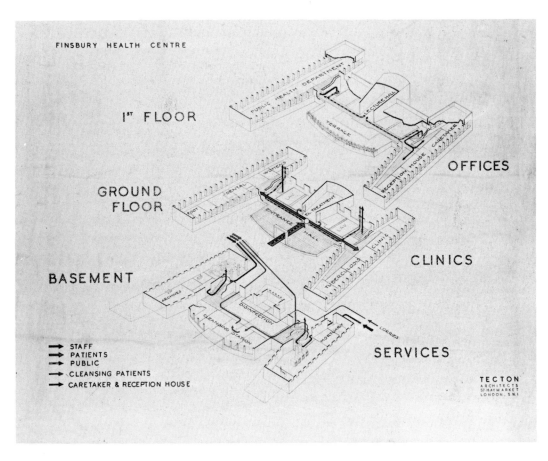

75 Tecton. Finsbury Health Centre

Education Buildings

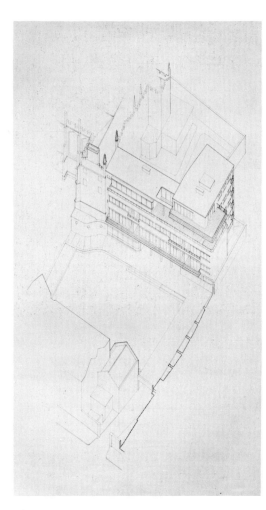

76 Maxwell Fry. New Fellows' building at All Souls' College, Oxford. Axonometric. Pen (1245 × 735)

In 1937 a Schools competition, promoted by the Liberal-progressive *News Chronicle*, attracted entries from Wells Coates and Denys Lasdun, Tecton, Breuer and Yorke, Raymond McGrath and Oliver Hill. It was won, however, by the 26 year old Dennis Clarke Hall, and as a direct consequence he was commissioned to design the Girls' High School at Richmond, Yorks (now listed). Yorkshire and Cambridgeshire were the leading education authorities – and the difficulty they had in offering 'progressive' patronage is shown by the fact that Henry Morris, the Cambridgeshire Director, was able to offer the Impington Village College job to Fry and Gropius only on condition that Jack Pritchard and his friends guaranteed (i.e. raised) Gropius' fee.

Oliver Hill designed a number of schools in Yorkshire in the late 30s, one of which, Whitworth Mere near Castleford, is now listed. His design for Methley Senior School at Rothwell, 1938-9, was not, however, executed. Seen at Plate 10 in a perspective by J.D.M. Harvey (1895-1978), the two main blocks are low, flat-roofed, with rounded ends, and all classroom windows are full-length glazed and sliding. It would hardly be apparent on the ground that the plan is aircraft-shaped, but such a plan had a functional advantage in separating the larger, classroom, block from the rear block of gym, art room and library, with the Assembly Hall in the linking 'fuselage'.

In 1934, the year which saw his move from Paris to London, Ernö Goldfinger designed an ingenious expanding nursery school (Plate 11) but he found no backers. He was more fortunate in the patronage of Paul and Marjorie Abbatt, the toymakers; for them he designed a showroom and shop, a flat, scaled-down children's furniture, and exhibition stands. The theme of childhood, for an architect not overburdened with commissions and with a growing family, was not surprising. Thus he also designed the 'The Child' display for Hill's 1937 British Pavilion in Paris and the 'Mother & Child' exhibit for the MARS group exhibition in the following year (fig. 97).

The 30s was not a striking decade for university building. Fry and Gropius did a rejected scheme for Christ's College, Cambridge, and in 1937 Fry was invited to submit designs for a new Fellows' building at All Souls', Oxford, probably on the prompting of the historian Richard Pares. The ramp in the foreground of his design (fig. 76) forms the entrance from the High Street to a proposed underground car park – for the traffic problems of the High were already apparent. Stone faced and extensively glazed, the uncompromising design did not commend itself to the college. There was probably some natural feeling that it would be out of keeping with its particularly august surroundings. Food for thought if so, as it would have taken its place in a group already happily spanning four centuries, from St Mary's Church and the Old Schools to Gibbs's Radcliffe Camera and Hawksmoor's Gothic towers for All Souls' itself.

There was nothing up to the minute about Sir Giles Scott's New Bodleian Library of 1935. In their 1931 Report the Bodleian Commissioners had stated that the new site should meet the University's book needs for two centuries, or at least for one. An oddly loose timescale, but no one concerned with libraries will be surprised that in the event space problems were acute again within thirty years. After his success with the Cambridge University Library, Scott was commissioned by Oxford too. His building, seen here (Plate 12) in a perspective by Lesslie K. Watson, had to be in scale with Hawksmoor's Clarendon facing it across the Broad and with the early 17th century unity of Wadham to the east. Scott achieved the modesty of scale called for, but he adopted the rubble-walled round-cornered effete manner widely employed in Oxford by Sir Hubert Worthington and Sir Herbert Baker, and the result has never been regarded as a successful addition to the University's architecture.

77 David Pleydell-Bouverie. Ramsgate
Municipal Airport

The Lure of the Machine

In 1934 Raymond McGrath published *Twentieth Century Houses*, an account of 128 buildings, two-thirds of which, despite the title, date from between 1930 and 1934. It is written in Basic English as a literary counterpart to the spareness of modern architecture. His many quotations, from Ruskin, Morris, the Prince Consort himself, are rendered down into Basic, though the originals, perhaps rashly, are printed, in all their verbal suppleness, in an Appendix. Basic English comes into its own, however, in the Last Words [*sic*]; 'The future is in the hollow of our hands. In the wide windows of the twentieth century house are framed the white towns of tomorrow... what other road is there to take but into these surprising distances?' The passage has a visionary ring paralleled in Le Corbusier's own writing, and still more in the disturbing blend of excitement and unease in Rex Warner's novels and the Auden-Isherwood plays.

A design of his own which McGrath illustrates is for a house to be named Rudderbar, at Hanworth Airfield, Feltham (1932). The year before, the Hon. Mrs Victor Bruce had commissioned Oliver Hill to design the house. She was an intrepid sportswoman to whom no mode of transport was alien, providing only that it was dangerous and exciting. She held a startling number of world records, in cars, speedboats and aircraft, and for her solo flight from India to Indo-China had been awarded the notable honour of the Order of the Million Elephants and White Umbrella.

Hill's work went ahead smoothly at first, and in January 1932 he wrote to her: 'I am building a new Hotel at Morecambe,' (see Plate 23) 'and am arranging a very long flat roof so that you can fly me there without coming to earth'. But by the end of the month mounting costs compelled her to tell him not to proceed further. However, she was still developing ideas of what she wanted at Rudderbar, and when later in the year she asked McGrath to take over the design its character was governed by some unusual conditions. She was about to make an attempt on the world record for staying aloft. As she took off, the first brick was to be dropped (literally) from the air. The building,

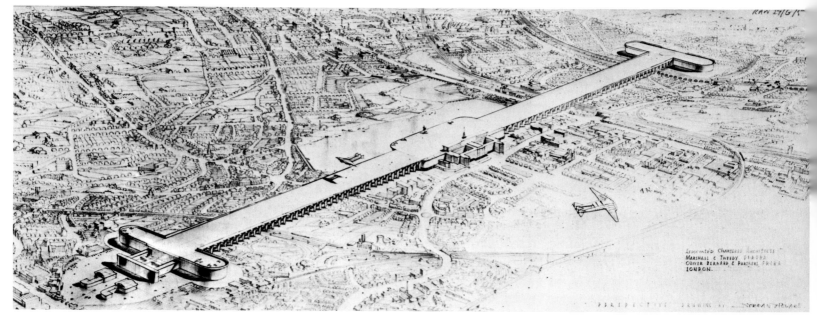

78 Marshall & Tweedy. Hendon Airport.
Unexecuted. Aerial perspective. Print of original
drawing (215 × 585)

steel frame and brick, with mosaic facings, was then to be erected, at a speed which would have
won McGrath some kind of record also, so that on her return to terra firma she would find a
house waiting and a hangar to put her plane away in. 'Why this did not come off', says McGrath,
'is a long story'. Unhappily he does not tell it. Mrs Bruce confirms that she did drop the brick, but
adds that 'the house was never built owing to my work for the government, which suddenly
greatly increased, so that I was unable to go on with the project.'

Aircraft had an absorbing appeal for the intellectuals of the 30s. The helmeted airman is a
predominant image in the work of Auden and Isherwood. The writings of Saint-Exupéry, dealing
in almost mystical fashion with his life as a pilot, were widely admired. Malraux, hero of the Left as
intellectual and man of action, was a fighter pilot in the Spanish Civil War. And in 1935 Le
Corbusier published, in England but not, curiously, in France, his *Aircraft*, a vatic hymn to the
flying machine, which epitomised the exhilaration and awe with which the aeroplane was to grip
the imagination of 20th century man. His darting mind also saw architectural significance: 'By
means of the airplane, we now have proof, recorded on the photographic plate, of the rightness of
our desire to alter methods of architecture and town planning.'

Wells Coates, who had flown with the RAF during the war, and Raymond McGrath were both
to design, though not to execute, aerodromes in the 30s. Two notable airfields were built by
modernists, Christopher Nicholson's Dunstable Gliding Club and David Pleydell-Bouverie's
Ramsgate Municipal Airport, now demolished (fig. 77). With its wraparound glazing and its
overhung roof surmounted by jaunty modern rails, in plan his building is gently swept back in the
shape of an aircraft's wings. In those pre-radar days it could all be agreeably simple in character,
and the whole central section had French windows which folded back to allow the public rooms,
the lounge and the tearoom, to be open to the air. No surviving photograph seems complete
without the two figures on the roof. They are probably not statues, but officials coaxed into giving
suitable scale to the camera.

The aircraft motif had already been used in 1931 by McGrath in his interior for the National Flying Services in Trafalgar Square, where the counter, supported on struts, was shaped like an aircraft's wings. And in 1932 he designed the interiors for Imperial Airways' Atalanta aircraft.

A number of other aerodromes, notable among them that for Birmingham by Norman and Dawbarn in 1938-9, were built in the 30s. One which remained unbuilt was the curious project for a runway by Marshall and Tweedy with Oliver Bernard, and drawn here (fig. 78) by Norman Howard. It is not known when or why the design was made, but the configuration of road and rail and the presence of the Brent Reservoir beyond the main airport building in the centre establishes that the project was for Hendon. It did not appear in the RIBA's exhibitions on Aerodromes (1932) or Airports and Airways (1937), but everything about it suggests the mid-30s. Note, lower right, the eight-engined twin-fuselaged aircraft circling the extraordinary giant runway raised on stilts (and apparently provided with no hangars or servicing buildings). It may have been a response to the 1933 Airports Conference, for which the Automobile Association produced *Towards Municipal Airports*, with its assertion that 'Foreign commercial aircraft are already attaining speeds of nearly 200mph. British manufacturers could make such aeroplanes if they did not have to be flown from small fields.'

It was not only aircraft which exhilaraté d the moderns. In *Vers une architecture* Le Corbusier had made much play with images of the Delage car and the liner *Aquitania*. Maxwell Fry, in a 1979 paper given before the RIBA, looked back to his early days in Liverpool, where he had an older friend and patron who was a great shipowner. 'Climbing up and down the cavernous engine-rooms of his ships lying in dock I first recognised the purposeful elegance of machinery, fortified by a boyish worship of the great steam locomotives which long trial and error had brought to a

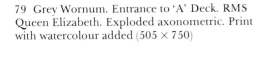

79 Grey Wornum. Entrance to 'A' Deck. RMS Queen Elizabeth. Exploded axonometric. Print with watercolour added (505 × 750)

80 Charles Holden. Arnos Grove Underground Station, London

pitch of powerful but unassuming beauty.' Blomfield disagreed. 'The engine of a French express can do its seventy or eighty miles an hour... but it is about as unsightly and squalid an object as i would be possible to find'. (*Modernismus*, p.72). Here as elsewhere he was going against the tide. I music Honegger's *Pacific 231* (and in a jazz a whole body of sung blues catching the desolate poetry of the locomotive); in the cinema Jean Gabin in Renoir's *La Bête Humaine*; these run in a straight line to our own age's nostalgia for steam. Like the aircraft, the locomotive was felt to be a once a potent symbol and a practical expression of the ideals of modern architecture.

Oliver Hill and Brian O'Rorke both designed interiors for de luxe railway trains, but the ocean liner was still the supreme way of transport. O'Rorke's interiors for the Orient Line's *Orion*, 1935 (Plate 3) and *Orcades*, 1937, were hailed by Paul Reilly (C.H. Reilly's son and later a distinguished Director of the Design Centre) in the *DIA News* for September 1937 as 'the best British examples of ship decoration since the early days of ocean-going liners, because they are the simplest'. Fitness for purpose, that most familiar of design catchphrases, here means literally shipshape; 'there is no pretence here that passengers are still in the Hotel Metropole. They are afloat and between decks'. The public rooms were decorated by McKnight Kauffer, John Armstrong, Ceri Richards, Lynton Lamb and Marion Dorn. Grey Wornum had also moved on, after his RIBA building, to the design of liner interiors, and figure 79 shows his 1938 scheme for the A Deck entrance on Cunard's *Queen Elizabeth*.

The most pervasive design style in transport sprang from the patronage of Frank Pick, Vice-Chairman of the London Passenger Transport Board. A founder member of the DIA, he established a corporate identity for London Transport which included the bull's eye station signs by Edward Johnston, posters by Paul Nash, Moholy-Nagy, Sutherland, Rex Whistler and McKnight Kauffer, and the standardised series of station designs which were predominantly the work of Charles Holden (1875-1960). Pick had already used Holden to design London Transport's Headquarters at 55 Broadway, 1927-9, with decorative work by Epstein, Henry Moore and Eric Gill. In 1930 he travelled with Holden (later the architect of the massive London University in Bloomsbury) through Scandinavia, Holland and Germany to survey recent architectural developments, and the next five years saw Holden's extensions of the London Underground system to the north and west. Arnos Grove, 1932, (shown in figure 80 miraculously free from traffic) displays one of his clean geometrical structures, concrete with brick infill, flat-roofed, metal-windowed, which, with so much else of the Pick-inspired house style, remain familiar to Londoners today.

Shops

In the early 20s P. J. Westwood (1878-1959), in partnership with Joseph Emberton from 1922 to 1926, began a long association with the tailors Austin Reed. This was to produce a restrained up-market house style which contrived to be in tune with the modern commercial world, and was to appear in many major cities over the succeeding decades. Westwood's pencil perspective (fig. 81) shows his 1931 frontage for Austin Reed in Birmingham.

Another architect who worked for familiar high street shops like the outfitters Montague Burton, Boots the Chemists, and (with the Russian-born designer Misha Black) for the café chain Kardomah, was Fritz Landauer (1883-1969). If, as seems likely, it was in 1933 that he emigrated from Germany, where he had had a substantial practice centred on Munich, his design for the street facade of Boots in Regent Street, 1933 (fig. 82) must have been among the first of his English

81 P.J. Westwood. Austin Reed's shop,
Birmingham. Perspective. Pencil (350 × 440)

commissions. The job was not executed along the Moderne lines suggested by his perspective,
and indeed it is hard to see how the obdurately traditional Boots logo could have been
comfortably incorporated into a contemporary design.

Altogether more welcoming than his Hammersmith Town Hall (plate 9) was Berry Webber's
prize-winning but unbuilt design for Daniel Neal's clothes shop in High Street Kensington,
1930, seen here (plate 13) in H.L.G. Pilkington's presentation. Webber's building was markedly
eclectic, set between two tiny flanking towers, with nine thin double-storey windows, each topped
with a baroque gesture, its stained glass lights between the five semi-circular glazed arches
surmounting the main street level display windows, and its pergola'd roof garden.

London's most notable 30s stores were Simpson's, Piccadilly, by Joseph Emberton, 1935-6, and
Peter Jones, Sloane Square, by William Crabtree with Slater & Moberly and C. H. Reilly, 1936-9.
Crabtree (b.1905) had worked for six months in New York with Raymond Hood in 1928,
subsequently joining Emberton's office; his signature as joint draughtsman appears in Emberton's
Olympia design (Plate 21). In 1930 he became for two years Research Architect to the John Lewis
Partnership, thereafter establishing his own practice.

In 1936 the Partnership commissioned him to design their new Peter Jones store in Sloane
Square. Reilly acted as consultant, and the old-established practice of Slater & Moberly looked
after the working drawings and contract supervision. 'I am but a small if entirely consenting

82

83

84

82 (*Facing page*) Fritz Landauer. Boots the Chemists, Regent Street, London. Perspective. Charcoal & pencil (755 × 365)

83 (*Facing page*) William Crabtree, with Slater & Moberly, and C.H. Reilly. Peter Jones Store, Sloane Square, London

84 (*Facing page*) William Crabtree. Peter Jones, Sloane Square, London. Perspectives. Pencil (380 × 245 & 210 × 245)

Plate 15: Gilbert Scott. Battersea Power Station. Preliminary studies. Pencil on tinted background. (635 × 510)

Plate 16: H.S. Goodhart-Rendel. Hay's Wharf, London. Elevation. Pencil & watercolour (590 × 495)

85 H.S. Goodhart-Rendel. Hay's Wharf,
London. Preliminary design of landward front.
Perspective. Pencil (635 × 430)

partner', wrote Reilly in his autobiography *Scaffolding in the Sky*, (1938), p.287. 'The real author of it is my dear old student William Crabtree.' One direct contribution of Reilly's, however (as Crabtree told the author), was the idea of curved ceilings in the shop windows to reflect the light (fig. 83). Crabtree's original sketch designs (fig. 84) show how elegantly he has taken the building round the curve of the street line. Its broad horizontal bands of opaque glass are played off against a continuous series of slender uprights framing unusually narrow vertical windows. Crabtree's coloured perspectives were submitted to the Royal Academy and rejected out of hand as having a shop for their subject. But the undated and rather breezy character of his building has always won it affection.

Another set of shop designs in the BAL are Raymond McGrath's for a Polyfoto studio in Regent Street, 1934. Polyfotos were a popular and effective way of having your picture taken. 48 different exposures were made at high speed and printed up at hardly more than postage stamp size. Then the ones selected were enlarged to look like posed studio portraits.

McGrath's design (Plate 14) shows the company preparing to move up market. There was now to be a waiting lounge complete with bar and mirrored sidewall – the room is in reality half the size it appears to be – and the idiosyncratic skill of his draughtsmanship flatteringly suggests a glamorous ambience in which no-one need hurry, and where, sipping your Gimlet or your Bronx, you would be in the company of *flâneurs* as languidly elegant as yourself. Alas, it was not built.

Industrial and Transport Buildings

While the Moderne factories of Wallis Gilbert & Partners were reaching out along the Great West Road, two powerful RIBA Presidents were doing important industrial or commercial work on London's South Bank: Giles Gilbert Scott, PRIBA 1933-5, at Battersea Power Station, and Goodhart-Rendel, PRIBA 1937-9, at Hay's Wharf. Battersea had a complicated story. Already in May 1929, the President of the RIBA was writing to the Prime Minister expressing alarm at the risk from noxious gases to old buildings 'if the proposed erection of immense Electric Power Stations in the heart of the Metropolis is allowed to proceed' (*Architect & Building News*, 17 May 1929). But the risk was taken, and only when the engineer S. L. Pearce's scheme was fully evolved were the architects Halliday and Agate called in to clad the structure. Later still, in 1930, Scott was appointed consultant to make their exterior design acceptable on a dominating site which gazed across the river at Pimlico in the heart of London.

There was no existing British vocabulary for this quintessential machine age building type, and Scott had to labour to devise an appropriate statement within a configuration already fully determined. His was the fastidious and subtle brickwork with fluted chimneys (Plate 15 shows one of his sketch designs), and his the Moderne detail, including much use of glass, marble, decorated tiles and bronze-doored lifts with Art Deco bas-reliefs, most of it wholly unseen by the public at large.

As architect, public figure and scholar Goodhart-Rendel was always his own man. His Head Office for the Hay's Wharf Company, 1930-32, produced a building which must have surprised thousands of commuters down the years as their trains pulled into London Bridge Station, and given them some pleasure, too, standing there like a handsome stranger in the heedless wreckage of the area. Clad in Portland stone on a steel frame, it was raised on stilts, not for any fashionable reason but to answer the needs of riverside unloading. The symmetrical river front (Plate 16) had a central framed section decorated with faience reliefs by Frank Dobson, behind which stood the Directors' Common Room and, above it, the double height Board Room. Figure 85 shows the landward front in a preliminary perspective. The main features are all present, but as built the block was a storey less in height, and Goodhart-Rendel replaced the mild little lid of the perspective with a more dashing top floor, the fenestration of this quite different and the central body surmounted by white tubular railings.

Another major industrial work by Scott was the Guinness Brewery at Park Royal, 1933-6 (fig. 86). Here again is his impeccable brickwork, with the north and south fronts of each block relieved by projecting fluted verticals rising the full height and a vertical ribbed motif running right round each just below roof height. At Park Royal Scott firmly followed his own precept of 1933: 'Let us avoid being too extreme, even if it does pay in these vulgar days to be sensational.'

The best known of all his work, apart from his GPO telephone kiosks, was the new Waterloo Bridge, 1932-45. In 1924 it was found that Rennie's much loved bridge of 1811-17 was subsiding, and years of controversy followed between advocates of rebuilding and preservationists like Lethaby and Blomfield. But Herbert Morrison, the powerful leader of the London County Council, was determined to press ahead, and Scott was brought in. Construction work began in 1937, two lanes were opened in 1942 and the completed bridge was opened in 1945 by a triumphant Morrison, by then a cabinet minister. Among Scott's preliminary designs in 1932 was a vast monumental structure (seen in figure 87, looking north), with huge paired towers at either end, complete with frieze. Happily, while the politicians wrangled, he worked on at further designs, less offensive to Chambers' Somerset House, its neighbour to the north east, and finally evolved the low-cut grace of the present bridge.

86 Gilbert Scott. Guinness Brewery, Park Royal, London

87 Gilbert Scott. Waterloo Bridge, London.
Preliminary design. Perspective. Pencil
(650 × 770)

88 A.G. Sheppard Fidler. Aqueduct and viaduct
over a gorge. Student design. Plan, elevation,
section & perspective. Pencil (1020 × 690)

A river crossing not subject to the constraints which faced Scott was a bold 'Aqueduct and viaduct over a gorge' by A.G. Sheppard Fidler (b.1909). This plan, elevation, section and perspective (fig. 88) was a sketch design done while he was a fourth year student at Liverpool, and inscribed 'Mention CHR [eilly] 28 Jany 1932'. In his autobiography Reilly recalls Sheppard Fidler as 'a hard-working, logical, clever, intelligent fellow, who never made a bad plan. He not only won the Rome, but also the Victory Scholarship, that is to say, the first and the second of the great prizes open to all British subjects for architectural designs.' (*op.cit*, p.210).

The last industrial building shown here (Plate 17) is Oliver Bernard's Vickers Supermarine works at Hazel Road, Southampton, 1935-7, in a presentation finely evocative of its period by Robert Myerscough-Walker (b.1908), one of the best of all the architect-perspectivists. Boldly horizontal in line, with characteristic semi-circular glazed staircase and stainless steel balustrading, the works fronted onto the river Itchen. The main hangar opened by means of a huge counterbalanced steel door, and the greater part of the office block and several of the works buildings were erected on reclaimed land. By mid-decade the tilt towards war was already having a wide impact on architectural practice. Bernard was no longer working simply on Corner Houses and popular hotels. In November 1935 he wrote in *Building*: 'Am getting on with the reconstruction of an Aviation Works, getting ready for some more King and Country. Nobody wants to serve in or see another war, but disarmament is like saying, "it ain't goin' to rain no more". Supposing it does rain after all...'

89 Wamsley Lewis. New Victoria Cinema, London. Interior

Cinemas

In 1928 the first Talkies arrived in England and gave an impetus to the building of a whole series of new cinemas. In what were often fairytale interiors architects now had to provide not only luxury, escape and warmth but also good acoustics. It was no good trying to guess from the outside what the foyer or auditorium might look like, and many exteriors, despite some forays into Moorish, Egyptian, Chinese and even Jacobean styles, were very ordinary, some frankly dull.

In town centres large cinemas were naturally more ambitious, and one of the finest was the.New Victoria, Vauxhall Bridge Road, London, by Wamsley Lewis (in partnership with W. E. Trent), begun in 1928 and opened in 1930. After spells in the offices of Stanley Hamp and Goodhart-Rendel, Lewis (1898-1977) won the RIBA Bossom Scholarship in 1927 and studied theatre design in Germany and New York for a year, setting up in practice on his return as a direct result of an invitation to design a 'Super Cinema' at Victoria.

Plate 18 shows a preliminary design for the Wilton Road elevation of the New Victoria. There are minor differences from the final treatment, but the essential horizontal bands, enclosing horizontal windows, which give the building its Mendelsohnian character, are already strongly present. Close inspection shows that the lettering on the fascia of Lewis' watercolour reads: 'Fishy great new comedy smelly film finest illuminated stage show in the metropolis the Victoria'; and the film announced, 'The Hour of Gladness with Greta Garbo', is not one known to historians of cinema. This firm modern façade gave no clue to the fantasy within. In the auditorium the patron, who had very likely entered in the dark, found himself as the lights slowly came up, in a mermaid's palace of innumerable stalactite lights (fig. 89).

Many of the new cinemas were not new at all but revampings of already extravagant buildings stranded by the decline of the music hall. The Empress Brixton by Andrew Mather (1890-1938) is a case in point. Starting life as the Empress Theatre in 1898, it closed during the 1914-1918 war, and was not re-opened until 1931, when it was extended and altered, no doubt to capitalise on the Talkie boom. In 1933 it became the Granada, and it is now, like so many others, a bingo hall, though the interior is largely unaltered. Shown here (fig. 90) are two alternative preliminary designs for the auditorium, entirely different in character from each other and demonstrating the freedom to fantasise which the designers (outside the Odeon chain) enjoyed.

In the mid-30s Mather became, with George Coles and Harry Weedon, one of the three principal designers for Odeon, and in 1937 he worked with Weedon as consultant on the group's 'High Command' cinema, the Odeon Leicester Square. Weedon (1888-1970) had designed his first cinema in 1912 at Perry Barr in Birmingham. After a varied practice there in the 20s he became early in the new decade interior design consultant to the cinema magnate Oscar Deutsch for his Odeon Theatres – the title a punning play on Deutsch's initials – and, soon after, consultant architect with ultimate responsibility for all Odeons. The Leicester Square cinema, seen at Plate 19 in a preliminary elevation, had not yet acquired what Hugh Casson ten years later was to call 'its monstrous club-foot' thrusting into the London sky. The final design, produced in Mather's office, was largely the work of Thomas Braddock, later to be a Labour MP. The cinema was built on the site of the old Alhambra of 1854, which had been used as a Biograph for moving pictures before the turn of the century. In the First World War it was the home of the Byng Boys and in 1921 of the Diaghilev Ballet. Deutsch made no attempt to create dream interiors, settling for simple economical lines with an unmistakable Art Deco sweep but free from the fuss Art Deco so often fell into. The great number of Odeons built from about 1934 onwards were carried

90 Andrew Mather. Empress Cinema Brixton.
Interior perspectives. Pencil & crayon
(each 350 × 250)

through with military precision and timing. They were built at breakneck speed, often by casual labour and otherwise unemployed craftsmen. The larger ones took a year or less to complete, the smaller ones seven or eight months. Weedon's lieutenant and successor Robert Bullivant recalls that the title of the film to be shown on opening night was sometimes announced before construction started and when shooting on the film itself was only beginning. This speed was achieved by Weedon's establishment of much standardised detail, from projection rooms and sales kiosks to exit signs and ashtrays. Equally, and here the shining black rectangles in Leicester Square lacked many of the Odeon's most typical hallmarks, he provided the exterior house-style which, once settled, made for speed of design and construction. The external elements included flowing horizontal curves ('streamlining') played off against predominantly rectangular masses, with a tall fin or tower displaying the Odeon sign in standard lettering, which carried the eye down the cream-tiled façade to the entrance canopy. The Odeons also learned from the Berlin cinemas of the 20s the excitement created at night by leaving a building in darkness apart from a few carefully chosen features brilliantly picked out in neon lights.

International Exhibitions

We have seen how, apart from domestic houses, few openings offered themselves to the modern architect. There were occasional victories in public building competitions – Mendelsohn and Chermayeff's Bexhill Pavilion (figs 119 to 121) is the leading example – but such contests were generally won either by traditionalist figures like Vincent Harris and Berry Webber or by half-way designs strongly influenced by Sweden or Holland, such as Pierce's Norwich City Hall and Wornum's RIBA Building. Department stores and shops, Crabtree's Peter Jones, Emberton's Simpson's, provided further opportunities in a field where Mendelsohn's series of Schocken stores in Germany had blazed a widely admired trail. But for the most part the modernists were confined to interior design (where, behind a conventional exterior if need be, the modern could flourish without public affront) and, very importantly, to exhibition work.

The ephemerality of exhibition design worked in the architect's favour. Rather as the animals in the zoo were clients who would not argue precedents with Tecton so the temporary nature of exhibitions did not force their designers into solemn conventions but allowed them to experiment, and to learn from the results against the time when more lasting jobs came along.

The story was different when heavy-handed official taste was responsible. The British Empire Exhibition at Wembley in 1924 had been a profoundly conservative affair, a self-applauding display of 'the might, dignity, power and prestige' of the Empire (*Official Guide*, p.237) 'The material chiefly used...[was] concrete with stone. No lesser foundation would serve the purpose of the Empire' (*ibid.* p.13). Such a pageant of Empire underlined obliquely, as did its artefacts directly, Britain's insular lack of concern with the new waves sweeping over Europe. It was not unreasonable that this should have been so; better surely, or so it must have seemed, to hold to the road of imperial prosperity than to throw in our lot with a Europe ravaged by war and smouldering with revolution. And what was good for the country economically seemed quite satisfactory to the arbiters of official aesthetic taste, however much the Design and Industries Association might wring its hands.

In the following year the Exposition des Arts Décoratifs took place in Paris, the exhibition which gave its name to Art Deco. It has come to be seen, and rightly, as a seedbed for so much in the

Moderne manner which was to flourish over the next decade. But this was a by-product. The intention, like that of Wembley, was at heart chauvinistic. It was to be a showcase (to which Germany was markedly not invited to contribute) for French design, and a reassurance that after the interruption of the war elegance and luxury were back in business in Paris.

The exhibition is remembered, architecturally, for buildings quite untypical of the pervasive chic, for Melnikov's Soviet Pavilion, Goçar's Czechoslovakian Pavilion and for Le Corbusier's Pavillon de l'Espirit Nouveau – significantly the Ministre des Beaux Arts entertained such grave doubts about the latter that he kept it closed, relenting only at the eleventh hour. The singular British Pavilion by Easton and Robertson, who were also to do the British Pavilion at the New York World's Fair fourteen years later, was untypical in a different way. The British contribution was in general poor. There was all too little government money for displaying British arts to Europe; manufacturers had to buy their own space, and opportunities were largely missed.

In its coverage of Expo the *Architectural Review* ignored Le Corbusier's Pavilion, and the exhibition as a whole rates no mention in J. M. Richards's *Introduction to Modern Architecture* (1940). He reserved his praise for the Stockholm Exhibition of 1930, for which Gunnar Asplund was the architect. This was the first opportunity, apart from smaller displays like the Stuttgart Weissenhofsiedlung of 1927, to see modern architecture consistently displayed over a wide area, and here with a grace and craftsmanship, a lightness of touch and a lack of dogma, which were to have a profound effect on young British architects.

Among these was Oliver Hill, who became a kind of master of ceremonies to British 30s exhibitions. Among much else he was architect to the 1933 Dorland Hall exhibition of British Industrial Art and to the 1934 exhibition of Contemporary Industrial Art in the Home; and he designed the British Pavilion at the Paris International Exhibition of 1937. The roll call of those he selected as collaborators in the exhibitions he supervised was a striking one. Among the architects were Chermayeff, Coates, Fry, Connell, Ward and Lucas, Emberton, McGrath, Maufe, Robertson, Sisson, Tecton; among the painters and decorative artists Ivon Hitchens, Kauffer, Dorn, Ravilious and Bawden, and he was for ever casting out his net, not always with success. He had used Gill at his Morecambe Hotel, but he could not secure him for his Paris Pavilion. Gill's letter to him of 7 October 1936 makes very plain his attitude to such festivities: 'Forgive me if I put it briefly and bluntly: I hate these international exhibitions, the raison d'etre of which is the boosting of foreign trade. I hate this sham medievalism of royal coats of arms, especially when attached to modernistic industrialism. That is enough for the moment. I believe you really will understand.'

Hill was a natural choice for the 1937 Paris Pavilion. His steel framed building was white rendered, with areas patriotically picked out in red and blue, the whole composition showing his characteristic play of rectangle against cylinder. J.D.M. Harvey's perspective (Plate 20) shows the benefits of employing a first-rate illustrator. Critics found Hill's design bland, and a waste of the best space in the exhibition. Not everyone was inspired either by basketwork displays and a giant cutout of Neville Chamberlain fishing. Nearby, competing with each other in megalomaniac inhumanity, were the monstrous pavilions of the USSR and Germany, the latter designed by Albert Speer.

Among the decorators Hill used here were Ravilious, Kauffer, John Nash, Bawden, Goldfinger and John Skeaping, who besides designing the Royal Arms over the recessed portico did a frieze 171 feet long. It can be seen marching off the edge of Harvey's perspective. But the most memorable exhibit of all in the exhibition was in the Spanish Pavilion, by J. L. Sert: Picasso's *Guernica*.

Rondo Capriccioso

Hill, who liked to design every detail of his buildings, the furniture, the door knockers, the decorations, even the maids' uniforms, was instrumental in setting up in 1930 a private company named Rondo to display and market the best in modern decorative art. Debarred by his professional status from any business interest in the company, he was its consultant architect and its moving spirit, getting Lance Sieveking, for instance, to write its publicity. A letter from Wells Coates (fig. 91) offers collaboration in the project. It shows how the true modernist was beholden to Hill as ringmaster; three years later it was Coates who proposed the exclusion of Hill, together with Howard Robertson, Grey Wornum and others, from the newly formed MARS Group as being among those 'certain people...popularly and notoriously known as "modern" architects [who] obviously do not qualify in our sense' (Cantacuzino: *Wells Coates*, 1978, p.47).

Coates's letter was doubtless typed at his special mobile desk which, in tune with his concern for the Minimum Flat, stored away into a wall when not in use. He had his own style typographically as in other things, employing asterisks (in red) where a run of the mill typist would be content with full stops, and starting each new paragraph with a paragraph mark. Though his suggested collaboration with Rondo did not come about, his letter has a further interest in its conchusion. This statement of his credo, with a quotation which he used on a number of occcasions, shows his pride in having grown up in a society where the cultured man is not an onlooker, a novel reader and gallery goer but (as he was later to write) 'one who is himself an artist of living: one who has been trained sensually to the aesthetic apprehension, who inherits a culture perpetually resurrected in his own eyes, voice, hands and movements' (*ibid*, p.11).

It was Rondo which was to sponsor the celebrated Ariadne's Bath for the Pavilion of Light at the 1930 Ideal Home Exhibition. The bath itself was of fluted honey-coloured Botticino marble, the bathroom walls of translucent Egyptian onyx lit from behind, the ceiling glass backed with gold leaf. This supreme extravagance seriously alarmed the elderly baronet whom Hill had persuaded to be Chairman of the Directors. His alarm turned to outrage at Hill's unusual ideas for publicising the bath, and things turned into farce with an apoplectic challenge over who it was had ordered from Fortnum & Mason's, and who was to pay for, a powder puff, a pair of dumbbells and a skipping rope. Rondo ended in bad blood; but the bath itself found its way into the Neo-Georgian North House, Westminster, which Hill designed for Robert Hudson, MP. Taken on its own, the Rondo Affair might have been devised by Evelyn Waugh; and one owes it to Hill to record that his exhibit at the Ideal Home Exhibition in the following year was a village for maladjusted children.

Trade Exhibitions

Figure 92 shows the changing letterheads of the 1933 Dorland Hall exhibition. The earliest is more suited to an established solicitor's office than to a forward-looking presentation of industrial design. It is soon transformed by the use of Leon sanserif, symmetrically laid out, and develops into its final form with a squarer face and an elongated coloured logo.

Besides the familiar architect names on the Executive Committee there were four artists and designers in Paul Nash, Harold Stabler, Gordon Forsyth and Noel Carrington; there were Hastings of the *Architectural Review*, the writer Holbrook Jackson, Goldsmith of the BBC, the gallery

Plate 17: Oliver Bernard. Vickers Works,
Southampton. Perspective by R. Myerscough-
Walker. Watercolour (380 × 735)

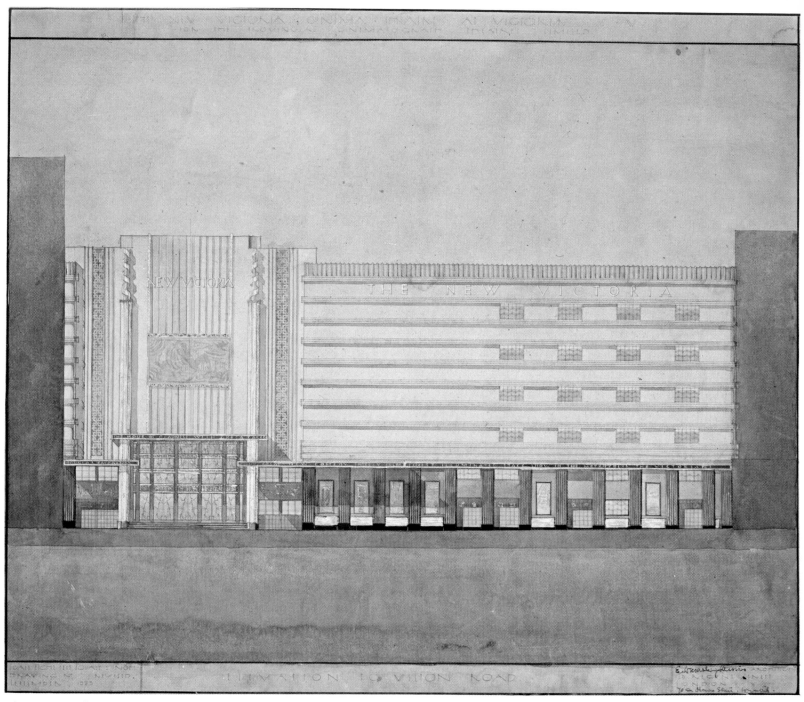

Plate 18: Wamsley Lewis. New Victoria Cinema,
London. Print with pen, pencil & watercolour
added (550 × 660)

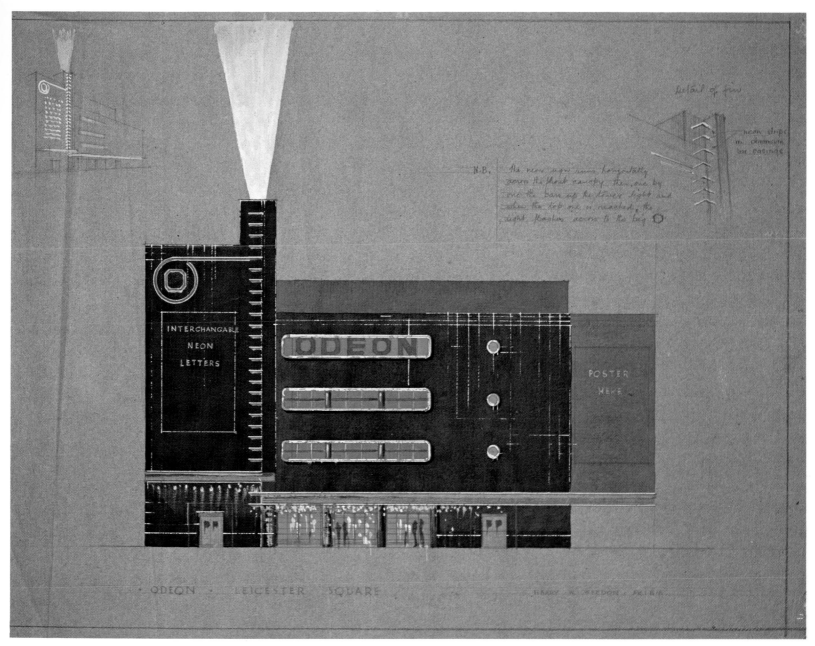

Plate 19: Harry Weedon. Odeon Cinema, Leicester Square, London. Preliminary elevation with sketch detail & perspective. Pencil, crayon and gouache (475 × 625)

Plate 20: Oliver Hill, British Pavilion, Paris
Exhibition 1937. Perspective by J.D.M. Harvey.
Pencil & watercolour (565 × 760)

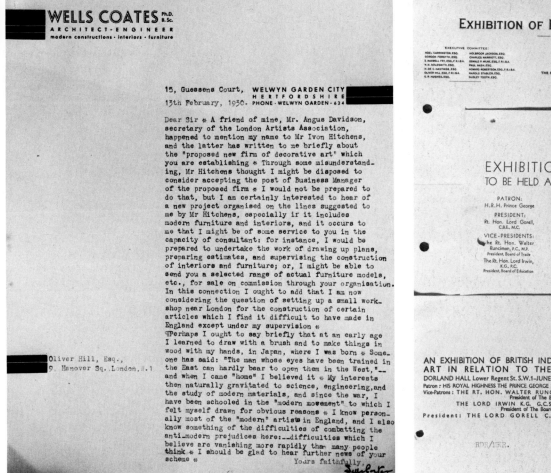

91 Wells Coates. Letter to Oliver Hill,
13 February 1930

92 Successive letterheads of the Executive
Committee for the Dorland Hall Exhibition, 1933

owner Dudley Tooth, the art critic Charles Marriott and G. R. Hughes, Clerk to the Goldsmiths'
Company and thus the controller of powerful patronage. The Chairman was the architectural
historian Christopher Hussey, whose systematic accounts of English country houses in the pages
of *Country Life* throughout the decade have overshadowed the memory of his vigorous involvement
in promoting modern design.

In Hill's working design for 'The Equipment of the Home' stand (fig. 93) can be seen, bottom
right, the section allotted to Chermayeff for 'The Week End House' and, top left, the Minimum
Flat which Wells Coates designed for Isokon. The exhibition aroused great interest, and attracted
30,000 visitors in just over three weeks.

Another architect whose gifts were much in evidence in exhibitions of the period was Raymond
McGrath. In 1938, for instance, he participated both in the Building Trades Exhibition, where he
designed the stands for James Clarke and Company (fig. 94), and in the Women's Fair at
Olympia, presented by Odham's Press. Some of the features of this Fair would not hold great
appeal for feminists - beauty preparation displays, beach wear in the Hollywood Gardens,
conversation pieces in the Fashion Theatre with actresses as mannequins – but there were nearly

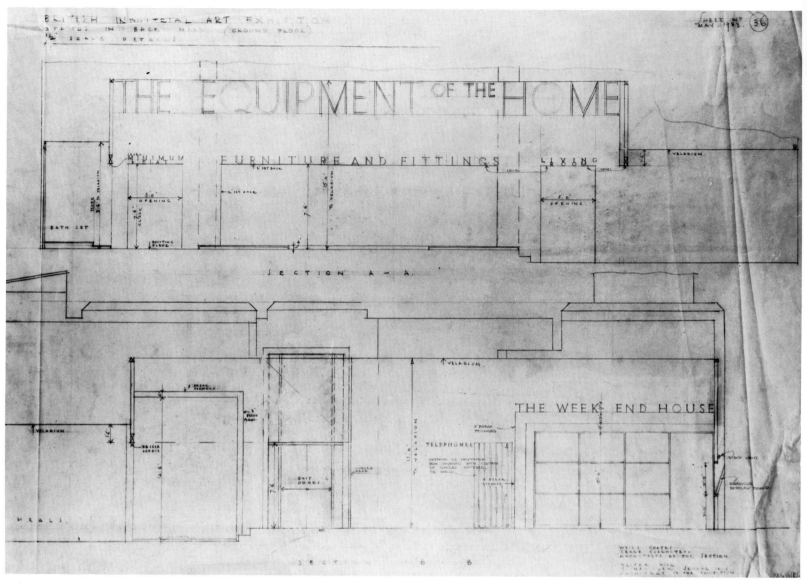

93 Oliver Hill. Design for "Equipment of the Home" stand, Dorland Hall Exhibition 1933. Details. Pencil (675 × 990)

half a million visitors, and an important section was organised by the DIA. Superintending architect for the overall layout was J.E. Lansdell of Beresford Marshall & Partners, and the prize-winning central feature, to illustrate the importance of design in domestic objects, was by H.T. Cadbury-Brown, who had been a main organiser of the RIBA's Small House exhibition earlier in the year. In design terms the outstanding display was the electrical industries stand by McGrath, highly characteristic in its transformation of the modest space available to him by means of curved planes and decorative planting schemes (fig. 95). An ironic postscript to the exhibition was the distress caused in right-thinking circles by a comprehensively vulgar Scottish 'Clachan' of tartans and tweeds, 'completely ruining the appearance of the main gangway...the presentation was appalling and yet the public simply adored that exhibit; and who can say, therefore, that the exhibit was wrong?' (*DIA News*, Jan 1939, p.4).

94 Raymond McGrath. Stand for Building Trades Exhibition, 1938. Perspective. Pencil (255 × 445)

95 Raymond McGrath, Stand for Women's Fair Exhibition 1938. Perspective. Pencil (340 × 560)

GENERAL VIEW OF MAIN HALL   E.D.A. STAND . WOMENS FAIR . OLYMPIA 1938   RAYMOND McGRATH B.ARCH A.R.I.B.A.

The Women's Fair had been held in the decade's major exhibition site at Olympia, where the New Empire Hall, 1929-30, was the work of Joseph Emberton. It is seen here (Plate 21) in a presentation perspective by P.G. Freeman and William Crabtree; Emberton himself owned to an almost total lack of ability when it came to draughtsmanship. In 1933 he extended Olympia, and in 1935-7 designed for it a garage holding 1200 cars, in Maclise Road, claimed on its completion to be the largest garage in Europe. Everything was clearly and elegantly to the point in this brick-faced structure with its continuous sweep of horizontal glazing (fig. 96).

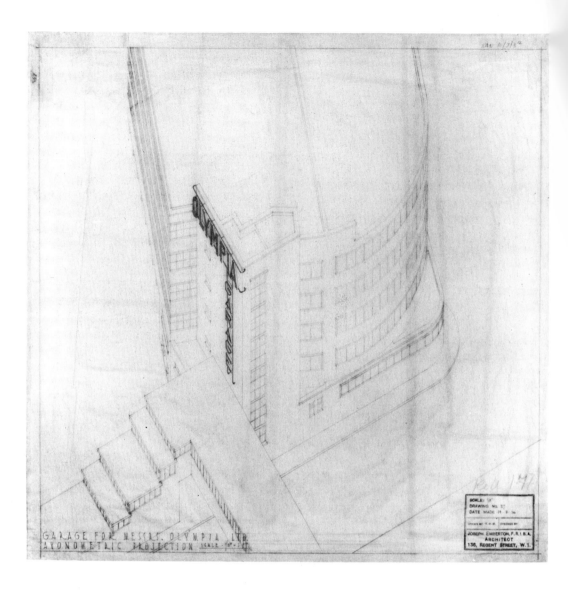

96 Joseph Emberton. Olympia, London:
Garage. Axonometric. Pencil (480 × 520)

The Mars Group

Most of these 30s exhibitions, which gave so welcome a shop window to the modern designer,
were intended to promote trade, industrial art, domestic furniture and the like. But there was one
significant display to promote modern architecture itself; that of the MARS (Modern Architectural
Research) Group. This was the most substantial gathering of the modernists against whom
conventional society's doors seemed barred, or at least by whom society was determined not to
have its doors designed. Met by uncomprehending hostility or, just as bad, plain indifference, they
naturally felt themselves isolated. They had chauvinism to contend with too. Those who noticed
them at all sometimes regarded them as spreading an alien and very possibly Bolshevik poison
over the land. So they banded together.

In 1930, prompted by Mansfield Forbes, the Cambridge don who had given McGrath his first job, the Twentieth Century Group was formed, with Wells Coates, McGrath, Chermayeff, Jack Pritchard, Etchells and Howard Robertson as originating members. As is the way with such groups, it was short-lived. The same fate befell Unit One in 1933. This was a group of nine painters and sculptors, including Moore, Hepworth, Nicholson and Paul Nash, and the architects Wells Coates and Colin Lucas. An exhibition was held at the Mayor Galleries in April 1934; it subsequently toured; a book was published to which each participant contributed; but distintegration followed, hastened by a drive from Wells Coates and Paul Nash to put far more stress on to the applied arts. Its impact, apart from the book, was negligible.

More important (though in truth none of these groups was of towering significance) was the MARS Group. Sigfried Giedion, the Swiss Secretary of CIAM, the Congrès Internationaux d'Architecture Moderne, had approached Morton Shand to form a group to represent England at future Congresses. Shand, oenologist and influential publicist for modern design – it was he who persuaded Pritchard to invite Gropius to England – enlisted the eager help of Wells Coates, and the MARS Group was founded. Coates was Chairman, Fry Vice-Chairman, Yorke Secretary, and other founding members comprised Connell, Ward, Lucas, Samuel and Skinner (of Tecton), Pleydell-Bouverie, and four non-architects, all stalwarts of the *Architectural Review*, Shand, Hastings, John Gloag and Betjeman. This was in 1933. Later in the decade (and the Group lasted until 1957) they were joined not only by other leading modern architects such as Chermayeff and Lubetkin, but by publicists for progressive ideas such as Raymond Mortimer, Herbert Read, Commander Goldsmith of the BBC and R.S. Lambert, editor of *The Listener*.

Their aim was to identify the problems of modern architecture and to move towards their solution. It was never altogether clear what the Research of the title should consist of beyond the stimulus of discussion. There was neither the breadth of technical knowledge nor the testing facilities (nor, for that matter, the time) to carry out serious research into basic questions like damp proofing or the right use of new materials. But the cause, for faith rather than works was the driving force, got under way with the *Architectural Review* acting, in MARS Group member John Summerson's phrase, as 'the Diaghilev of the English architectural stage'.

They set up a number of committees, (Legislation, Schools Propaganda, Lectures, Housing, Building Costs among others) which served as forums both for the exchange of ideas and for developing a sense of corporate solidarity. In unity is strength, or at least reassurance. The trouble was that an effective pressure group needs far more unity than MARS could provide. Under the banner of its belligerent title was a variety of viewpoints. And as commissions increasingly came to the leaders they naturally moved from the debating chamber to the drawing board and the building site. But they had one great boost. Just as they were starting, the emigrés were arriving from the continent, and a prospect opened up that the modern movement might acquire a significant corpus of work rather than mere isolated essays 'towards a new architecture'. The emigrés, men rooted in the real world of modern European design with substantial achievements behind them, must have been walking messages of optimism to the young and insular English architect, so remote in his working life from the successes of modernism in Europe.

MARS was not merely an inward-looking collection of theoreticians. They had a keen sense of public relations; indeed, on occasion their letters to the press were too inflammatory to be published; and they ranged widely. When Paxton's Crystal Palace was burned down in November 1936, they felt that a great symbol not only of the proper use of modern materials like glass and iron but also of the value of mass-produced standardised units, had been destroyed. They issued a statement that 'in losing the Crystal Palace, Great Britain has lost the evidence of her most important claim to have made an original contribution to modern architecture' (*Architects' Journal*, 10 December 1936, p. 821). Incidentially, Pilkington's, the glass manufacturers, always a lively patron of modern design, promptly announced a competition for a new Crystal Palace to show the possibilities of glass in the design of a modern exhibition hall. Among those who entered were Maxwell Fry, Raymond McGrath and Oliver Bernard.

In the following year came the MARS Group Exhibition, planned for June 1937 and finally opened in January 1938 at the New Burlington Galleries. It was intended, says the *Prospectus*, to offer an invitation to judge of the real nature of modern architecture and the part it will play in contemporary life. 'Now that the experimental stage is over there are enough examples to show the practical advantages of such buildings and the enjoyment that is to be derived from them'.

Until his departure for Chicago overall supervision was in the hands of Moholy-Nagy; then it was passed to Misha Black. Many of the members designed individual sections – figure 97 shows for, instance, Ernö Goldfinger's plan and perspective for the 'Mother and Child' section – and younger members took a hand too, Peter Moro and Gordon Cullen, for example, designing the entrance screen. The poster was by McKnight Kauffer, the catalogue introduction by, of all people, Bernard Shaw. The Tecton architect Godfrey Samuel hit on the idea of using Sir Henry Wotton's famous three 'conditions of well building', from 1624: 'commoditie, firmenes and delight' (fig. 98), and thus implicitly claiming a link over three centuries. The phrase was to be modulated, according to the *Architects' Journal* gossip columnist, by a distinguished guest, probably Robert Byron, as he departed from the grand reception, into 'Commodity, Guinness and Tonight'. John Summerson wrote, and intoned, what he later called 'captions and exhortations of the most vacuous pomposity'. It was a great event.

Le Corbusier himself descended from the heavens – 'on January 19th I dropped out of an airplane into the midst of a charming display of youth,' he wrote in the *Architectural Review* for February 1938. It must have seemed a shade provincial, even ingenuous, to him, but he wrote generously of it. In 'this magnificient exhibition' what struck him particularly was 'the elegance, the intimate eloquence, of its sequence of presentations, none of which could possibly alarm anybody' (a telling aside?), and the memory it left with him was of 'the lyrical appeal of those poems in steel, glass and concrete. The New Architecture can no longer be reproached with being mere insensitive and soulless technics.'

Although it ran only from 11 to 29 January, the exhibition made a considerable impact, attracted 7,000 visitors and amassed a vast deficit, which despite generous support from the industry had finally to be cleared by the executive committee itself, as the Account Books, presented to the BAL by Ove Arup (who was Treasurer at the time), make poignantly clear.

But time was passing. The pragmatism of some members and the sardonic wit of others were imposing strains on the Group's cohesiveness, while a new generation was emerging, austere and self-confident. Centred around a group of students from the Architectural Association, itself undergoing considerable turbulence at the time, they attacked the exhibition for its lack of overt opposition to the 'anachronistic social system'. It was these same critics, led by Anthony Cox, who took Tecton to task for the formalism of their Highpoint Two (figs 41 & 42).

The MARS Group had one more major offering: their Plan for London. Behind the plan was the Marxist emigré Arthur Korn, and there were to be no half measures. An east-west linear spine was to be created across London, with, north and south, a series of residential/commercial/recreational ribs, the whole encircled by a major ring road. Radical, visionary, totally impracticable, it would have involved massive destruction beyond the dreams of the Luftwaffe.

97 Ernö Goldfinger. MARS Group Exhibition.
Mother & Child section. Plan & perspective
details. Pencil (350 × 460)

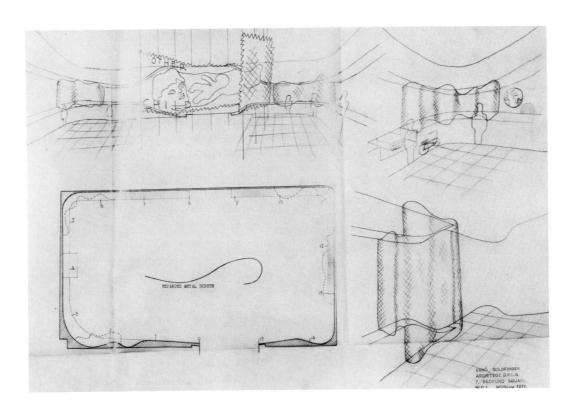

98 MARS Group Exhibition

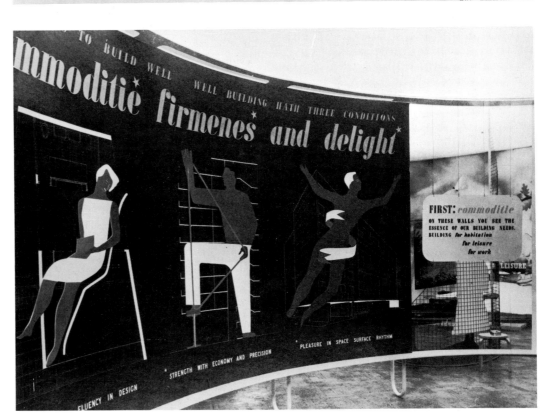

Recreation and Pleasure

The most popular manifestation of modern architecture in the 30s was probably Tecton's Penguin Pool at the London Zoo, 1933, a series of interlocking spiral ramps in concrete which provided a perfect stage setting for the antics of the penguins. Crucial to the technical achievement which this sculptural design represented was the great Danish engineer Ove Arup. He worked with Tecton on most of their major commissions, adding to his sympathy with their design aims the essential ingredient of endless technical resourcefulness.

Their first building at the London Zoo, in 1932, and their first association with Arup, was a house for two Congolese gorillas (fig. 99). Their solution was highly ingenious. The building was circular. One half formed the gorillas' living quarters, with clerestory lighting across the diameter. Through the other half circle, and inside the bars, a concrete wall could be swung in winter to enclose the whole, or swung back in summer to open the area to view, thus providing agreeable climatic conditions both for residents and onlookers (fig. 100). Opponents of modern architecture were sometimes heard to mock at a leading practice's designing some of its most spectacular work for penguins and gorillas rather than for their fellow men. Such cynicism was facile. Work for animals allowed an inventiveness, a free play of imagination, which would have stood no chance at all with local authorities. And the result was a triumph.

A more widespread kind of leisure building was the speciality of a now neglected architect of the interwar years, Oliver Bernard (1881-1939). His career was a notable one even leaving out of account his work as an architect – and he contrived to write an enjoyable autobiography, *Cocksparrow*, with hardly a hint in it that he was an architect. By the age of 16 he was a scenery painter and an actor in Shakespearean repertory. Two years before the mast as a cabin boy on a tramp steamer and a spell as seaman on a Norwegian barque followed. He returned to the theatre, first as an assistant set painter at Covent Garden, then as Technical Director of the Boston Opera Company. By this time the war had broken out and he was determined to return, crossing the Atlantic, en route for enlisting, on board the *Lusitania*. He survived being torpedoed and served from 1916 to 1918 in France as a Captain in the Royal Engineers, emerging with a Military Cross. Back to the theatre as Technical Director for Beecham Opera and more set designs, one of which was realistic enough to blow up its creator while he was producing 'An Air Attack on London' at the Admiralty Theatre. He became a Technical Director at the Wembley Exhibition of 1924, and Consultant Artistic and Technical Director for the British Government's participation at the Paris Exposition in 1925.

Architecturally his fame rests on his work as staff architect to the caterers and hoteliers J. Lyons & Co. F. J. Wills was the architect of the buildings themselves, of the Cumberland Hotel, the Oxford Street Corner House, the Strand Palace, whilst Bernard was described as architect-designer for the public rooms. Here he created a series of interiors which constituted one of London's two great interwar building types designed for mass pleasure, in the popular West End hotels and the multi-storey cafés called Corner Houses. Unlike the cinema, the other characteristic type, Lyons Corner Houses had a unity of design created by Bernard, who combined decorative flair with technical inventiveness. If the spectacle, for spectacle was always his forte, lacked refinement, his profusely varied but always recognisable Art Deco interiors were exactly calculated for their clientele. With their reassuringly homely waitresses, or Nippies, they provided an easily accessible setting of opulence for shoppers up for the day, for office workers in the evening and for the young to talk the night away in, for the larger ones were open all night. The ambience he

99 Tecton. Gorilla House, London Zoo

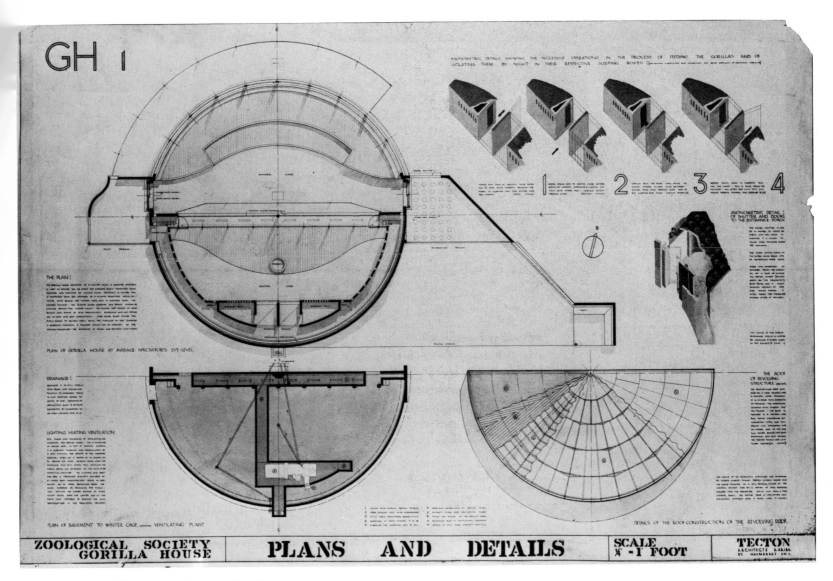

100 Tecton. Gorilla house, London Zoo. Plans &
axonometric details. Pen & wash (650 × 990)

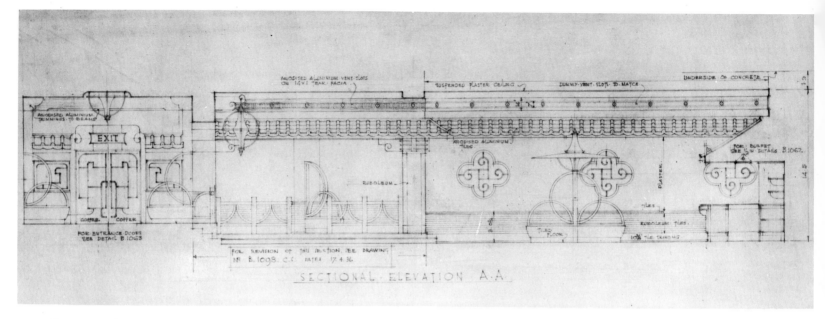

SECTIONAL · ELEVATION · A·A

101 Oliver Bernard. Lyons Corner House, Coventry Street, London. Section of interior. Pencil (detail from sheet 420 × 710)

created admitted ordinary people to an exciting and economical glimpse of life in the capital city. The preliminary sectional elevation of the restaurant interior for the Coventry Street Lyons, 1935-36, (fig. 101) is entirely characteristic of his work in its use of aluminium tiles and copper and above all in its decorative patterning.

Bernard worked for a marginally different clientele in his big hotels, slightly better off and more sophisticated without being in the least open to the charge of being fast. Again he was out to design interiors which communicated a sense of fun, a feeling that you were very definitely not at home but need not be nervous all the same. His cocktail bars are described in *Building* (May 1935) as 'just a trifle dissipated and naughty, but not sufficiently so to be vulgar', and his dishearteningly named Chez-Cup Bar at the Regent Palace Hotel is hailed as 'slick and smart and quite the last thing in interior decoration'. Figure 102 shows his scheme for the Lyonnaise Lounge, probably at the Regent Palace Hotel.

The Corner Houses have now gone, though a single revival has recently been installed at Charing Cross. Their owners must have come to think them *démodé*, and their death knell was sounded in the 1950s by the arrival of the Espresso machine and the multitude of ignoble snack bars and takeaways which in turn superseded the coffee bars and have paved the streets of London with litter.

Few of Bernard's professional colleagues would have thought highly of his cafés. They are a notable example of that extra dimension which the passage of time gives to some buildings. Time's accretions have established them as evoking their period so powerfully that a merit has been bestowed on them which was not evident when they were first designed. This is why his entrance to the Strand Palace Hotel has been acquired by the Victoria and Albert Museum as a significant piece of period design.

Altogether more fashionable than Bernard's Corner Houses was Fischer's Restaurant in New Bond Street, 1932-3, by Raymond McGrath. From the ground floor cocktail bar a curved and steel-balustraded staircase (fig. 103) swept down to a basement restaurant seating 150, with a dance floor and a platform for the band (Plate 22). McGrath's characteristic care over the

102 Oliver Bernard. Lounge for the Lyonnaise,
London. Perspective. Pencil & crayon (470 × 480)

PROPOSED·SCHEME·FOR·THE·LYONNAISE
PERSPECTIVE·SKETCH.   OLIVER·F·BERNARD·IRIBA
                                       ARCHITECT·90·PARK LANE·W.E

103 Raymond McGrath. Fischer's Restaurant.
Staircase

decorative lighting shows itself here in his use of 'sunlight' nitrogen tubes supplemented by
concealed cornice lighting which casts a tantalising play of light and shadow through the staircase
area, and signals anticipatory pleasure to the diner-out.

'Fischer's', wrote McGrath in 1972, 'suffered a conversion to the Tudor style some time in the
fifties, a style still popular in some drinking circles', a phrase which might have come straight from
an Anthony Powell novel, as Powell's characters would themselves have been absolutely at home
in McGrath's depiction of the original restaurant.

A curious recreational project for the later 30s was the design for a stadium and club on
London's Albert Embankment (fig. 104). The perspective, drawn by R. Scott Cockrill, and
exhibited at the Royal Academy in 1937, was very much in the manner of the American Hugh
Ferriss. The formidable building itself was designed by Alfred Ospalak (1899-1979) and his
brother David (1900-1976). The occasion of the design is not known; had it been executed its
towering height and massive proportions would have dominated London's riverside.

As to the traditional pleasures of the English public house, designs in the 30s staunchly reflected the conservative tastes of the drinking classes. A typical example is the Farmer's Hotel at Lancing (1935) by Stavers Tiltman (d. 1968), one of a chain of pubs done by him in Sussex, and shown here in a perspective made by E. J. Thring in 1938 (fig. 105). But a few architects made a clean break with Brewers' Tudor and Georgian. Among them was Oliver Hill with the Prospect Inn at Minster-in-Thanet, 1936-8 (fig. 106). Already by 1933 Hill was responding to a preliminary enquiry from Martin Thomson, the Ramsgate brewer: 'I shall be delighted to do your roadhouse, provided of course that it may be modern as distinct from imitation period.' The brewer replied that £3,000 was all they could spend in these hard times, and that his co-directors might feel that they would not 'get as much "building" for their money with Hill as with some lesser light'. Hill came back at once: 'I'll show you what can be done for £3,000. Your co-directors don't know what they might miss.'

104 A. & D. Ospalek. Stadium & Club for Albert Embankment, London. Unexecuted. Perspective. Crayon (625 × 470)

105 Stavers Tiltman. Farmer's Hotel, Lancing. Perspective by E.J. Thring. Pen & watercolour (520 × 695)

106 Oliver Hill. Prospect Inn, Minster-in-Thanet. Perspective. Pencil & crayon (330 × 665)

In the event the building was not completed for another five years. 'Planned as an outstretched butterfly' rhapsodized the *Brewer and Wine Merchant* in December 1938, 'at night, a fiery star on the roof gleams over the marshes'. Hill's massing of cubes and squat cones, his glazed semi-circular bars, his port-hole windows, show the high-spirited assurance with which he used modern motifs. The canopied open loggia on the west side must been irresistible to the summer motorist en route for Margate.

Hill would have been familiar with the work of E. B. Musman, the pioneer creator of a new pub style, and, significantly, among his earliest files on Minster-in-Thanet is a photograph of Musman's Nag's Head. In 1932 Musman had designed the famous Ace of Spades roadhouse at Surbiton, and the Nag's Head at Bishop's Stortford in 1934 is characteristic of his rejection of the ingle-nook and the horse brasses. Figure 107 shows his perspective of the preliminary design, white rendered, with a strong horizontal emphasis in its substantially glazed frontage and long low walls stretching away to either side to give the whole composition an added but wholly unostentatious presence.

107 E.B. Musman. The Nag's Head, Bishop's Stortford. Perspective. Pencil & watercolour (395 × 720)

108 E.B. Musman. The Comet, Hatfield

His most notable pub was the Comet at Hatfield, 1936. This was sponsored by the owner of the Grosvenor House Hotel in Park Lane, and named after the Comet aircraft built by De Havilland nearby in which Scott and Black had broken the speed record for a flight to Australia in October 1934. The front elevation (fig. 108) shows its family resemblance to the Nag's Head, and Musman's meticulous section (fig. 110) displays the disposition of spaces, from the paved outside terrace, in through the fully glazed opaque windows to the saloon with the service area, up through the sitting room and finally to the roof garden and octagonal glazed tower. Cosmo Clark, Gertrude Hermes and Musman himself were responsible for the interior decorations (fig. 109) with aircraft motifs everywhere, whilst Eric Kennington designed the sculpted column in the forecourt, surmounted by a model of the Comet.

109 E B. Musman. The Comet, Hatfield. Interior

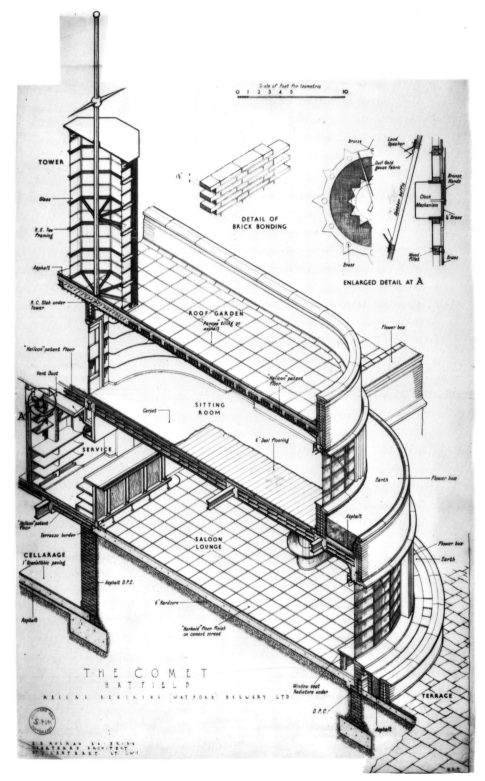

110 E.B. Musman. The Comet, Hatfield.
Axonometric section & details. Pen (885 × 540)

111 Edwin Lutyens. The Drum Inn, Cockington,
Devon. Aerial perspectives. Pencil & crayon
(each 255 × 440)

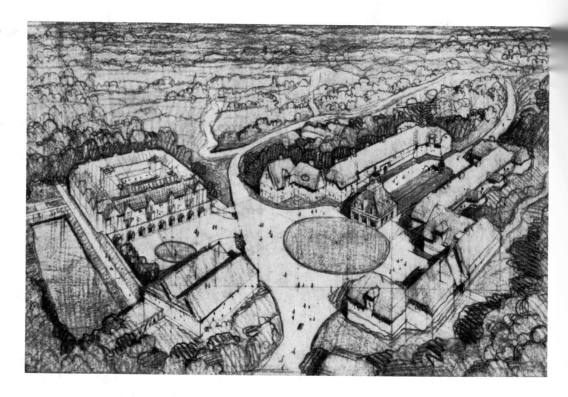

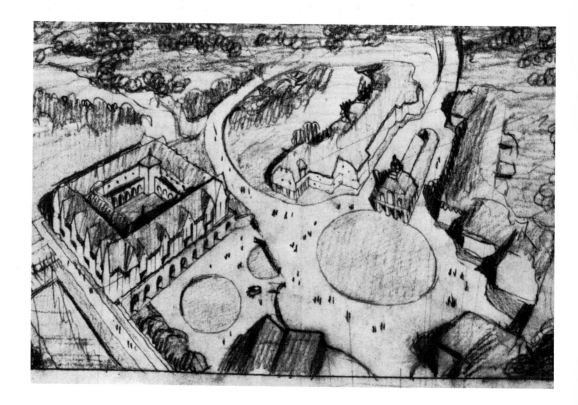

Plate 21: Joseph Emberton. Olympia, London.
Perspective by P.G. Freeman & W. Crabtree. Pencil
& watercolour (610 × 1300)

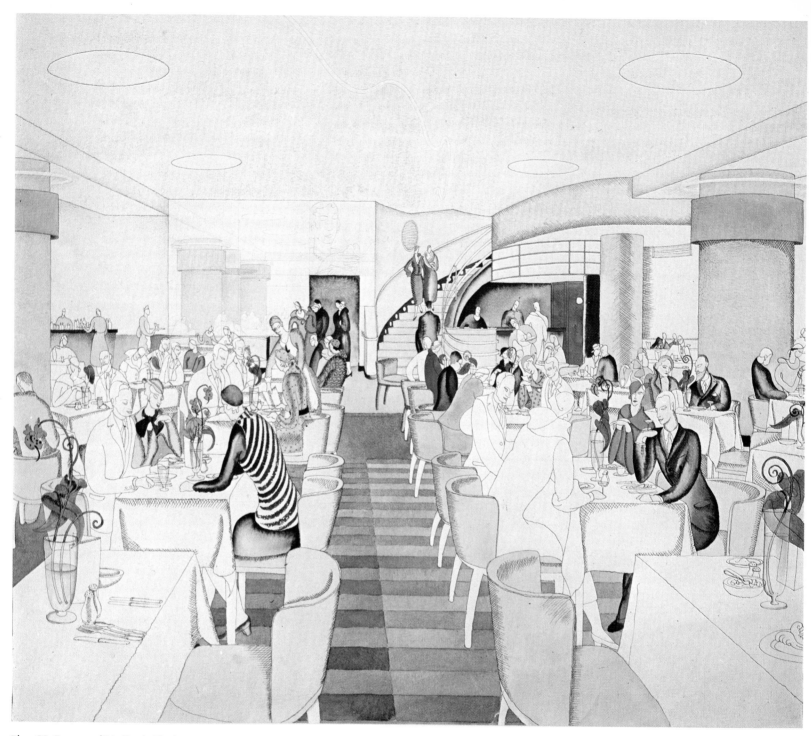

Plate 22: Raymond McGrath. Fischer's Restaurant,
New Bond Street, London. Interior perspective.
Pencil & watercolour (640 × 690)

Plate 23: Oliver Hill. Morecombe Hotel.
Perspective by J.D.M. Harvey. Pencil &
watercolour (525 × 1045)

Plate 24: Joseph Emberton. Blackpool seafront.
Perspective by Cyril Farey. Pencil & watercolour
(410 × 1040)

While the Nag's Head was being designed, Sir Edwin Lutyens (1869-1944) was working on a *jeu d'espirit* of an inn in Devonshire. He was at Cockington, near Torquay, to advise on the conservation of the beautiful village and to design the Drum Inn. The result was a highly picturesque pub with a thatched roof and exposed rafters in the bars which had light fittings on them in the form of brilliantly coloured heraldic beasts. In a letter of 1 August 1933 to his wife Lady Emily he describes his first visit to the area: 'Well it was all very amusing – and a little alarming. They have 7000 acres & most lovely country, & oh my they are laying it out with rows and rows of up & down miserable houses – they will be the slums of the future and as bad...Saw the village – an old spoil Hall – good church – remarkable trees – & a rough and tumble thatched village. My problem was to advise on the village, & to site & design an hotel, the village to be kept as a centre of attraction to the requirements of undrilled hovels...I made some sketches...' Figure 111 shows his first rough drawings of Cockington, where, incidentally, his fears about redevelopment were not in the event to be justified. The next day he went on to Dartington, the estate and the progressive school recently founded by the Elmhirsts. 'Infants (?) by an American architect, the school by Milne, cottages by de Soissons, and the Hall being restored by Schultz Weir. I said how weird... but you never saw so many chances missed.' The Headmaster's house, by the American Lescaze – 'new modern the most miserable house I ever saw – all talk and no house – looked about £2,000, but it actually cost £8,000. You cannot live without reflected light... You go blind without window bars whereon the mindless eye may rest...'

Modern Estates

The American architect William Lescaze (1896-1969) about whom Lutyens was so scathing was also the designer of a major private housing scheme planned for the south Devon coast at Churston Ferrers, in Torbay between Brixham and Paignton. Here in 1935 the Dartington Trust planned on 200 acres what was claimed to be 'so far the most ambitious attempt to build a comprehensive modern scheme to a uniform style'. Lescaze completed at least ten houses; the seaside hotel however (fig. 112) was not executed. It was to be a finely sited low raking building, but the scale in Lescaze's perspective is hard to master; either the cliffs are tiny or the people trudging up across the fields towards the western end of the hotel are of astounding stature.

Churston did not have the 'anthology' character of the estate at Frinton-on-Sea in Essex. Early in 1934 a property company bought a 200 acre site and set up the Frinton Park Estate. Frinton was traditionally a select resort, distinguished above all for its comprehensive lack of all the fun of the seaside, and the new estate took pains to do nothing to attract the vulgar. Plans were made for 1100 houses grouped round a central avenue with shops at one end and a luxury hotel facing the beach at the other. The houses were to be zoned according to style, with the best 40 acres reserved for 'houses of the most modern design'. Oliver Hill was the advisory architect. He was an astute picker of architectural and artistic colleagues. His associates in the exhibitions he organised show this, as we have seen; so does the array of talent to whom he allocated sites at Frinton, among them Wells Coates, Connell, Ward & Lucas, Emberton, Fry, McGrath, Mendelsohn and Chermayeff, Tecton and F.R.S. Yorke. Some of them must have found it hard to be indebted to an older man who was certainly not 'one of them'.

Frinton ran into difficulties both with the local authority – concrete, as so often, was the point of conflict – and with an inexperienced local builder. Hill's own stylish hotel (fig. 113) with his familiar curving plan and a swimming pool on a huge terrace leading to the beach was never built,

112

113

112 William Lescaze. Hotel, Churston Ferrers, Devon. Unexecuted. Perspective. Print of original drawing (485 × 715)

113 Oliver Hill. Hotel, Frinton-on-Sea. Unexecuted. Aerial perspective. Pen (285 × 750)

114 Oliver Hill. Houses, Frinton-on-Sea

and the only houses executed by 'the most progressive and enlightened of our young architects' before the onset of liquidation were designed by Hill himself (about a dozen of them), by Wamsley Lewis, Etchells, Howard Robertson, Marshall Sisson, and R. A. Duncan, teacher, writer and partner in Percy Tubbs and Son, who had designed the coach work for a magnificent car of Goodhart-Rendel's a few years earlier. Figure 114 shows one of Hill's houses. The full photograph, taken through an appropriately nautical porthole, with walk-on roles for motor cyclist and blazered tennis player is reproduced on page 143.

115 Oliver Hill. Morecambe Hotel

The Seaside

Hill's other major contribution to seaside architecture was his Hotel at Morecambe in Lancashire (1932-33). It followed the curve of the promenade, the convex side towards the sea, with a central circular entrance tower enclosing the main staircase, which was surmounted by a roof-level solarium and faced at the top with two monolithic stone sea-horses (in deference to the Morecambe Bay shrimp) designed by Eric Gill (fig. 115).

Hill took charge of every detail, maintaining a compact and uncluttered white façade, in brick rendered white and polished, Hill's standard practice when working in the modern manner, and punctuated at one end by a single storey circular glazed café (Plate 23). Inside he used a number of the artists who had been working with him at the Dorland Hall Exhibition. Gill did a large relief in the hall, of Nausicaa welcoming Odysseus, to symbolise Hospitality, a medallion on the staircase ceiling and an incised relief map of the district, whilst Eric Ravilious painted a continuous mural of Morning, Noon and Night round the café wall (fig. 116). Marion Dorn designed the carpets, there was a fresco by Edward Bawden in the Children's Room, and other artists included Allan Walton, Frank Dobson and (said the *Morecambe Visitor*) Duncan Grand. All worked under Hill's direction; and he designed even the grand pianos and the tethered indiarubber ball plugs for the washbasins, which *Country Life*, a shade easily pleased, found 'adorable'.

His correspondence shows that he needed all his considerable persuasiveness to carry with him his clients, the London Midland and Scottish Railway Hotel Services, for whom he was to work again on a lesser scale over the Euston and St. Pancras Hotels. So Arthur Towle, the Controller, writes in June 1932, agreeing that 'the café needs to be very modern as it will probably be used by

116 Oliver Hill. Morecambe Hotel. Café interior with frieze by Eric Ravilious

young people...but the bar will largely be used by members of the working classes on holiday in Morecambe...and we must not confuse them with the class of people who will be using the hotel.' We must, he says, walk with kings in the hotel but not lose the common touch in the bar; thus the decorations must not be 'too exotic'. Straight-faced, Hill deflects this in the briefest of notes: 'I completely agree with all you say, and will keep the bar very sober.'

In November Towle's uneasiness returns over Hill's intention to have coloured face towels: 'I am not satisfied that the clientele we are likely to get at Morecambe will appreciate too much of this kind of idea. We must not be too much influenced by what is done in what I may call the more artistic circles of London. Do not let us get too "precious".' This stings Hill who replies by return. 'As far as I am concerned, there is no chance of the hotel or its furnishings being "precious"...we have an unique opportunity of providing something worthy, without being in the least meretricious or precious.' But all went well in the event, and Hill's scrapbook shows how triumphant was the response of both lay and professional press when the hotel was formally opened in July 1933, though naturally enough it stops short of revealing the structural defects which were to assail the building the following year.

117 Joseph Emberton. Staircase of the Fun House, Blackpool

At the same time Joseph Emberton (1889-1956) was working on a major seaside development for nearby Blackpool. A member of the MARS Group though never closely involved in its ideological commitments, he had been in partnership in the 20s with P. J. Westwood, designing pavilions for the 1924 Wembley Exhibition and shops for Austin Reed, and was the author of such famous 30s buildings as Olympia (1930), Simpson's in Piccadilly (1935) and the bravura headquarters for the Royal Corinthian Yacht Club at Burnham on Crouch in 1930-31, the drawings for which are unhappily too fragile to reproduce here. At Burnham, with its portholes and its trim tubular handrails, Emberton was perhaps the first English architect to use the familiar nautical motifs of modernism. Cyril Farey's perspective of Emberton's preliminary scheme for Blackpool, including a Cyclone, a Pleasure Beach and a Capitol (Plate 24), shows that he succceeded without incongruity in providing a modern envelope for the traditional pleasures of the seaside, and through the window of the top-to-bottom glazed circular staircase of his Fun House can be glimpsed Blackpool's famed Big Wheel (fig. 117).

Some light on contemporary attitudes to the fun of the fair is found in Anthony Bertram's Pelican Special *Design* (1938), based on a series of BBC lectures. Bertram, novelist, playwright and publicist for contemporary design, restricts himself to 'what affects only those with incomes below £8 a week', and if today's reader is momentarily taken aback by this figure let him reflect that Bertram's book, handsomely printed in Times Roman with good margins and 32 plates, sold for sixpence, in modern currency tuppence ha'penny.

Architecture plays a prominent part in his discussion of design, and his book displays, more tellingly than the writings of the avant-garde, the unceasing social concern of the taste-makers. He has much praise for Kensal House and for Forshaw's Pit Head Baths (fig. 44) ('a colossal social experiment...an architectural solution to a new social activity which...far surpasses anything else being done in this country'), and his treatment of 'Pleasure Buildings' is particularly revealing. Writing at the tail end of a disorderly design tradition, he proclaims that 'austerity has become possible'. At the seaside we can 'allow ourselves fantasy, provided we keep clear of vulgar riotousness'. He instances Emberton's Blackpool, and comments that Dreamland at Margate, by Leathart and Grainger (1934: figure 118), 'is most respectable architecture'.

There is a striking presupposition here which emphasises the gap between the leaders and the man in the street. Respectability was not, after all, a prominent ingredient of most people's dreamland. They would not hesitate long between austerity and vulgar riotousness, which they might think just the thing for the sea front. But the didactic spokesmen for modern design had a missionary purpose – and the BBC and Allen Lane's Penguin Books offered them incomparable outlets. They were set on persuading the community at large to share their own preferences for good proportion and lack of ornament, for 'clean, light, athletic building'.

A building which met with Bertram's unqualified approval was the Bexhill Pavilion of 1934. Earl De La Warr, Mayor of Bexhill and Chairman of the National Labour Party, had instigated a major competition (with T.S. Tait as Assessor) for a seaside complex to include theatre, restaurant, bars, a dance floor and a promenade.

The competition attracted 230 entries, and a storm, or at least a disagreeable squall, arose when the winners were announced as the refugee Eric Mendelsohn and his partner Serge Chermayeff. Why, demanded the right, should foreigners take work from British architects? But, replied the left, the names of all competitors were completely unknown, even to the Assessor himself. The RIBA, said the *Architects' Journal*, had risen above petty nationalism; its generous and unqualified welcome was vindicated by the fact that the best design had won.

118 Leathart & Grainger. Dreamland, Margate.

119 Mendelsohn & Chermayeff. Bexhill Pavilion. Perspective showing the staircase. Pencil (125 × 170)

There was some hasty regrouping on the right when it was discovered that Chermayeff was a British citizen, an RIBA member and an Old Harrovian, and fire was henceforth concentrated on his partner Mendelsohn, a German Jew who had not enjoyed Chermayeff's advantages. Under the ironic heading 'Alien Architects invade Britain' the *Architects' Journal* (15 February 1934) reprinted an article from *Fascist Week*, written before the Bexhill results were announced and the more revealing for that, denouncing the 'contemptible and despicable betrayal of our own countrymen' by the RIBA in encouraging 'these aliens who have found it advisable to flee from their own land'. Lord De La Warr commented that the RIBA had told the Home Office that in welcoming so distinguished an architect as Mendelsohn it 'would be pleased and proud to consider him for the profession's highest honours if he applied for naturalisation'.

The Secretary of the RIBA prudently spelled out the sharp restrictions imposed on refugee architects who wished to practise in this country. James Burfoot, who with his fellow right-winger Marshall Sisson had submitted an elegant entry which was 'recommended for special merit', joined the outcry against Mendelsohn, and the row rumbled on, broadening into a discussion of the nature of Fascist architecture. In the *Architects' Journal* (19 April 1934) a leading member of the British Union of Fascists made it clear that the failure of modern architecture was largely due to 'the aggrandisement of individual liberty', with which he contrasted 'the wave of cultural regeneration which Fascism is bringing to Europe'.

Some of Mendelsohn's early sketches – seafront views, the interior glazed staircase, a preliminary plan – are seen in figs. 119 and 120. The design as built comprised to the west a plain concrete box for the theatre with windows at ground level only, and a lower two-storey block to the east, all glass, steel, glazed tile and sun deck, containing restaurant and cafés and uninterrupted sea views. The blocks were linked, and the connection made from the town side to the sea, by a broad central hallway enclosed by handsome projecting curved glass stairways (fig. 121).

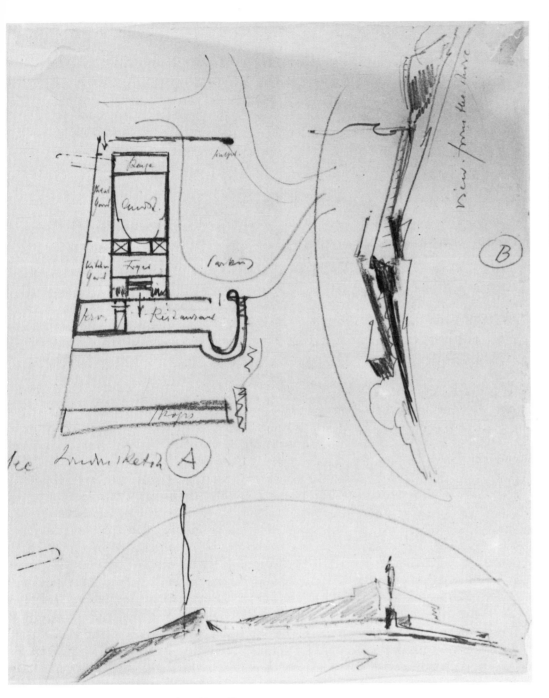

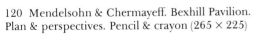

120 Mendelsohn & Chermayeff. Bexhill Pavilion.
Plan & perspectives. Pencil & crayon (265 × 225)

121 Mendelsohn & Chermayeff. Bexhill Pavilion

Refugees

This book is not the place for a detailed study of the profession's attitude to refugee architects, though the story deserves investigation. Already in 1933 the RIBA had proposed to the government that foreign architects with special qualifications and in a position to establish themselves in independent practice should be admitted. In effect this meant their entering into partnership with British architects. Thus Gropius joined Fry, his Bauhaus colleague Breuer joined Yorke, Mendelsohn joined Chermayeff. But despite Fascist objections ('we have been affronted by the spectacle of prosperous British architects lavishing on these aliens, at big professional functions, encouragement which they conspicuously withold from the young architects of their own race', wrote the *Fascist Week* in 1934), the influx was always very small. In 1939 only 25 refugees held labour permits.

The situation became more acute after Czechoslovakia was overrun, and in June 1939 an RIBA Refugee Committee recommended that of 53 architects seeking to practise in Britain 'at least 18' should be allowed to do so. With E. J. Carter as organising secretary the Committee also sought placement for refugees in Australia, America, Palestine and elsewhere, and pursued other general humanitarian work. The architect MP Alfred Bossom wrote to Carter in July; 'It does seem a terrible pity that the other professional bodies cannot join you in being helpful in this awfully pathetic situation', and the Committee's papers show Carter heavily involved in trying to help not only the architects but also engineers, builders, designers, sculptors and other artists. A fund was opened, and many offers of hospitality, together with some guarantees of complete maintenance, were made.

The major figures did not find in England the opportunities their distinction merited and before the decade was out they had all departed, Mendelsohn to Jerusalem, though he kept on his flat in Highpoint, Gropius and Breuer to America like the emigré artists Gabo, Moholy-Nagy and Mondrian.

In February 1937 *The Times* published a letter from Sir Patrick Abercrombie, Charles Holden, Herbert Read, Ian MacAlister (Secretary of the RIBA) and W. G. Constable, Director of the Courtauld Institute of Art, himself about to emigrate to America. It lamented the failure to hold Gropius in England and announced a farewell dinner in his honour at the Trocadero (Julian Huxley Chairman, Carter organising Secretary, tickets 25 shillings, including wine). The guest list (fig. 122) formed a roll-call both of the progessive design establishment and of their sympathisers. Geoffrey Faber the publisher was there. So were Goldsmith and Lambert of the BBC, Arthur Upham Pope, who combined left wing politics with an unrivalled knowledge of Persian art, the scientists Huxley and C.H. Waddington, and H.G. Wells. Moholy-Nagy, Bauhaus teacher, photographer, designer, painter, produced a dashing menu card for the occasion (fig. 123).

During his two years in England from 1935 Moholy-Nagy did much poster and publicity work, for Imperial Airways, London Transport and Isokon among others, and he designed the window display when Simpson's store in Piccadilly by Emberton was opened in 1935. He also provided the photographs for three handsome books: Mary Benedetta's *The Street Markets of London*, John Betjeman's *Oxford University Chest* and Bernard Fergusson's *Eton Portrait*. A 1949 reprint of the illustrations in the latter has a engaging account of the Etonian Fergusson, a subaltern in the Black Watch who was later to be Governor General of New Zealand, wandering through Eton ('a lively experience') with his markedly unconventional companion. Fergusson admired Moholy's photographic gifts, but could not come to terms with his constructivist painting. 'He took me to

123 Moholy-Nagy, Menu cover for Gropius Farewell Dinner.

ALPHABETICAL LIST OF GUESTS

A
Professor Abercrombie	6
Mrs. Patrick Abercrombie	106
Dr. Thomas Adams	127
Mrs. Mary Adams	67
Mr. E. W. Armstrong	84
Mrs. E. W. Armstrong	102
Mr. Ove Arup	25
Mrs. Ove Arup	124
Mr. D. Ascoli	109
Mr. Ray Atherton	133

B
Mr. D. Betts	95
Mr. D. Betts's guest	96
Mr. Eric L. Bird	18
Mr. D. L. Bridgwater	93
Mrs. D. L. Bridgwater	22
Professor Lionel Budden	125

C
Mr. William Cahn	94
Mr. Noel Carrington	123
Mr. Edward Carter	57
Mrs. Edward Carter	51
Mr. Cyril Carter	42
Mr. F. Charles	112
Mr. Serge Chermayeff	53
Mrs. Serge Chermayeff	28
Mr. Wells Coates	64
Mr. J. M. Cohen	62
Mrs. J. M. Cohen	65
Mr. Willard Connely	55
Professor W. G. Constable	105
Mr. George Cooke	59
Mrs. George Cooke	122
Mr. Graham Cunningham	97
Mrs. Graham Cunningham	119
Mrs. E. Curtis	117
Mr. D. Curtis	116

D
Mrs. Hugh Dalton	32
Mr. W. Davies	121
Mr. Richard de la Mare	10
Miss Elizabeth Denby	128
Mr. T. Denman	103
Mrs. T. Denman	108
Mr. E. M. O'R. Dickey	129
Mrs. E. M. O'R. Dickey	54
Mr. J. G. F. Donaldson	74
Mrs. J. G. F. Donaldson	63

F
Mr. Geoffrey Faber	4
Mr. Alexander Farquharson	77
Miss Ellen Frank	35
Mr. Ernst L. Freud	46
Mrs. Ernst Freud	5
Mr. E. Maxwell Fry	83
Mrs. E. Maxwell Fry	88

G
Dr. Siegfried Giedion	66
Mr. John Gloag	17
Mrs. John Gloag	78
Mr. V. H. Goldsmith	79
Mrs. Ise Gropius	1
Dr. Walter Gropius	135

H
Mr. Val Harding	15
Mrs. Val Harding	58
Dr. R. Hargreaves	24
Mrs. Hargreaves	37
Mrs. Gillian Harrison	7
Mr. Ashley Havinden	39
Mrs. Ashley Havinden	82
Mr. G. Brian Herbert	111
Professor W. G. Holford	29
Mrs. W. G. Holford	9
Dr. Julian Huxley	●
Mrs. Julian Huxley	3

I
Mr. Gilbert Inglefield	20
Mrs. Gilbert Inglefield	115

J
Mr. R. T. James	92
Mrs. R. T. James	19

K
Mr. H. Kallenbach	21
Mr. B. Katz	120
Mr. C. J. Kavanagh	101
Miss Gertrude Kolman	56

L
Mr. R. S. Lambert	33
Miss Judith Ledeboer	80
Miss Jane Lidderdale	13

M
Sir Ian MacAlister	31
Lady MacAlister	134
Mrs. Edward Maufe	43
Mr. J. E. R. McDonagh	34
Mrs. J. E. R. McDonagh	100
Mr. Charles Marriott	131
Mrs. Charles Marriott	30
Mr. Basil Marriott	99
Mrs. Hartley Mason	45
Mr. J. Duncan Miller	23
Mrs. J. Duncan Miller	71
Professor L. Moholy-Nagy	72
Mrs. Moholy-Nagy	132
Mr. Henry Moore	47
Mr. Henry Morris	70
Mr. H. G. Murphy	87

N
Mr. Christopher Nicholson	38
Mr. Max Nicholson	12
Mr. Clifford Norton	14
Mrs. Clifford Norton	104

P
Dr. N. Pevsner	61
Miss M. E. Pheysey	126
Dr. Arthur Upham Pope	16
Mr. Fleetwood C. Pritchard	89
Mrs. Fleetwood C. Pritchard	41
Mr. J. Craven Pritchard	36
Mrs. J. Craven Pritchard	69

Q
Mr. Hugh Quigley	90

R
Dr. M. Rachlis	86
Mr. A. B. Read	40
Mr. Herbert Read	68
Professor C. H. Reilly	44
Mr. Paul Reilly	60
Mr. J. M. Richards	11
Mr. Michael Ross	50
Mr. Gordon Russell	52

S
Mr. Godfrey Samuel	48
Mr. P. Morton Shand	8
Mrs. P. Morton Shand	26
Dr. S. Sieghein	76
Mr. J. Dixon Spain	118
Mr. C. D. Spragg	98
Mrs. Cunninghame Strettle	110
Mr. John Summerson	27
Mr. Cyril Sweett	113
Mrs. Cyril Sweett	91

V
Mr. R. Vaughan	114
Mrs. Dorothea Ventris	75

W
Mr. C. H. Waddington	49
Mrs. C. H. Waddington	73
Sir Alexander Walker	107
Lady Walston	130
Mr. Richard Weininger	85
Mr. H. G. Wells	2
Mr. Clough Williams-Ellis	81

122 Guest List for Gropius Farewell Dinner, 1937

an exhibition of his work in that field, and I thought there must be something wrong with me'.

Moholy designed another menu card for a farewell dinner. This time it was for Marcel Breuer, off to join Gropius at Harvard, as Moholy himself was about to leave to start the short-lived New Bauhaus in Chicago. The dinner was held in the Isobar of Lawn Road Flats, which had been converted from the original kitchen into a residents' club by Breuer and Yorke. The farewell dinner to its architect must have been one of the earliest uses it was put to.

Lubetkin Takes The Temperature

What was the situation these distinguished emigrés left behind? The first fine careful rapture was over. It no longer seemed imperative to reproduce the works of the European masters without regard to local conditions. Traditional materials, stone, brick, timber, were increasingly replacing reinforced concrete, which was ill-suited to what Fry called 'our moisture-laden, lichen-growing climate', and some degree of ornament was returning, as Lubetkin's work showed, in the face of purist hostility.

As the modernists surveyed the scene they could point to some notable victories and to an appreciable – though in truth not a very substantial – body of work. Indeed, in one of the significant popularising books of the late 30s, *A Key to Modern Architecture* (1939), Penn and Yorke claimed that 'the best European work is at present being done in Scandinavia and England'. They were not alone in this view. Two years earlier the Museum of Modern Art in New York had found English work interesting enough to mount an exhibition, 'Modern Architecture in England', and in the introduction Henry-Russell Hitchcock, architectural historian and tireless advocate of modernism, wrote, 'It is not altogether an exaggeration to say that England leads the world in modern architectural activity.'

At the same time, to coincide with the New York exhibition, Lubetkin wrote a revealing assessment of the modern English scene in the *American Architect and Architecture* (Feb. 1937, pp.29-30). There have been considerable changes, he argues, in the last five years, 'enough to prove that the strangest reversals are not only possible but likely'. Conservative countries have advanced; progressive countries have retreated. 'In Germany, once the foremost country in constructive innovation, the prevailing political regime has banished modern constructional methods and the external characteristics of modern architecture. The flat roof has become the symbol of revolt, the mark of political unreliability; to design horizontal windows is to attract the attention of the secret police. A very similar attitude exists in Austria and central Europe. In Russia, on the other hand, any attempt to design buildings of a light and joyful appearance is interpreted as an attack on the proletariat, by depriving him of the monumental proofs of his new found material prosperity. France and Czechoslovakia have long been paralyzed by economic crises.'

Thus England, which has lagged behind for so long, now leads the world in the acceptance of new ideas. So far so good. But the rest of his article is devoted to examining why a fully mature modern architecture has not come about here. Most of the reasons he gives – a deeply conservative industry, outmoded building regulations, planning restrictions – have already been touched on earlier. Taken together with the failure to adapt European standards to English conditions, they have had the effect, he says, of distorting real aims and values. It is such a victory to get a flat roof past the local authority that it overshadows in the architect's mind the real nature of his conception. So many allowances have to be made (when one knows, for instance, that the obvious coarseness and over-emphasis in structural members is 'due to the local surveyor's abysmal lack of knowledge of reinforced concrete construction') that 'the only firm criterion is that of function, and we see a return to the functionalist doctrine, which was probably believed in less by its own originators than by any one of those who came after'. The need for a building to fulfil its purpose should be the starting point, not the ultimate criterion. As things stand, there is no basis for properly founded and energetic criticism, which is necessary both to educate the public and to help architects themselves to formulate a firm intellectual grounding for their work.

Lubetkin's taking the temperature of his time ends with the unconvinced hope that the way forward may be through the Architects' and Technicians' Organisation (ATO), which he himself had founded two years before with his Tecton colleague Skinner. Unconcerned with aesthetics, the ATO was an overtly political grouping (in contrast to the MARS Group), aiming to bring about the new society promised by science and to realise the architect's social responsibility. Although it was supported by the scientists Bernal, Waddington and Haldane and by the Editor of the *Daily Worker*, it was not a front organisation for the Communist Party, for its architect leaders disapproved strongly of the servile and sterile productions of Soviet architects. But its utilitarian concern for practical matters like mass housing provided, thought Lubetkin, 'a far more realistic and promising line of attack than any idealist grouping of modern architects can hope to be'.

But Lubetkin's own brilliant passage across English architecture was coming to an end. He had arrived from Paris in 1930, and by the end of a single decade his disenchantment was all but complete. He was to abandon architecture altogether soon after the war (though in 1982 he was honoured with the Royal Gold Medal for Architecture), and when in 1970 he came to look back at the pioneer buildings of the 30s he wrote, 'My personal interpretation is that these buildings cry for a world which has never come into existence' (*Architects' Journal* 11 March, p.595). Nor was he the only one, as the decade drew in, to be gripped by melancholia. In 1939, just before he left for America, Chermayeff examined 'the latest political developments' in the *Northern Architectural Students' Association Journal* (February, p.22) and bitterly concluded that 'little has been gained in our lifetime through technical ability or newly developed social conscience, for lack of opportunity to apply them intelligently, except possibly for the erection of shelters fit for heroes to survive in'.

Much else, of course, was happening while Lubetkin was examining the state of affairs in England. Baillie Scott was designing Clobb Copse (fig. 10). Tiltman's pub at Lancing (fig. 105) was to open the following year; so was Emberton's Casino at Blackpool (fig. 117). In 1937 cinemas were going up at the rate of nine a fortnight, and eighteen and a half million people paid an average of a shilling each to visit them weekly. Wells Coates was working on slum clearance in Bethnal Green, and the MARS Group exhibition was to open the following January. Outside architecture Anna Neagle was appearing as Queen Victoria, and George V was crowned. George Eyston, Malcolm Campbell and Jean Batten broke land, water and air records. The question mark was dropped from the title in the new edition of the Webbs' *Soviet Communism: A new civilisation?* (in A.J.P. Taylor's words, 'despite severe competition, the most preposterous book ever written about Soviet Russia'). And Guernica was bombed.

Air Raid Precautions

By 1938, Chamberlain's Munich meeting with Hitler, and the inescapable evidence in the newspapers of aerial bombardment and its effects in Spain, brought the subject of air raid precautions to the forefront. AASTA, the Association of Architects, Surveyors and Technical Assistants, which had succeeded Lubetkin's ATO, moved directly into an assault on government policy. Nor of course did the progressives have the field to themselves. The topic was examined, from a variety of viewpoints, in both the national and the professional press; by this time Oliver Bernard, for instance, was writing a regular column in *Building* on ARP and camouflage, drawing on his own experience in the First World War, and F. E. Towndrow, an architect sympathetic but not committed to the modernists, was signing an article in *Architectural Design* 'F. E. Towndrow, ARIBA, Assoc. Fellow ARP Inst.'.

The subject was shot through with bitter debate, about feasibility and cost and above all about the merits of surface as against deep shelters, and it was sharpened still more by reports of the German raids on Barcelona in March 1938, where (as John Langdon-Davies' *Air Raid*, 1938, documented in detail) the planes glided in silently and very low on reaching their target and caused considerable civilian panic.

Some of those who fought in the First World War (and they need have been no more than 40 years old at the end of the 30s) resented the radical solutions put forward by younger architects, whom they regarded as a motley crew with unattractive political motives. A rancid example of this appears in a private letter of 21 March 1939 from a much-liked architect to Goodhart-Rendel, the PRIBA. He derides the offer of a famous engineer to lecture on ARP, an offer rejected since 'a good deal of what he wanted to say was already well known...and he did not appear to know as much about the subject as he thought he did'. Engineers, who 'are very much inclined to look on it as a purely scientific problem...do a little random reading and thinking and they think they have discovered something which no one else has yet thought of...We happen to have got past that stage.' The bile spills over in a final paragraph: 'Have you observed two curious facts? First, that the majority of advocates of deep shelters are Jews, such as Lubetkin, Chermayeff and Samuely, and that to them A.R.P. is a matter of personal protection almost entirely. Second, that those who claim to have a scientific understanding of the subject also have no military experience. I have yet to find an old soldier who is an exponent of deep shelters.'

A variant view, but one likely to commend itself just as little to AASTA, came from Bernard. In reviewing Chermayeff's *Plan for ARP*, he pleaded for a little more humility, for some appreciation

124 Tecton. Design for deep air-raid shelter, Finsbury, London. Unexecuted. Section. Print of original drawing (detail from sheet 785 × 1050)

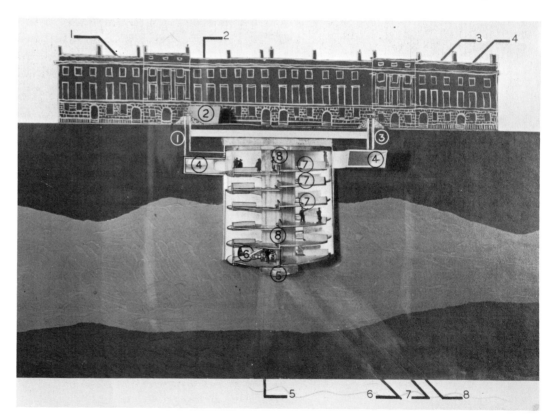

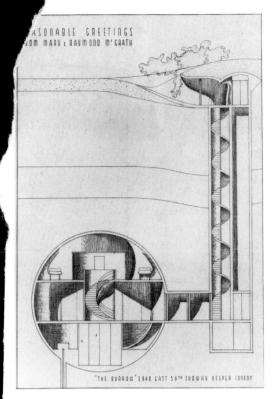

125 Raymond McGrath. Design for a Christmas card. Section. Pen (310 × 205)

of military problems, since ARP was, he said, an element in military strategy. Shelters, he concluded bluffly, are 'not an architectural prerogative. They are a straightforward problem in muck shifting at a requisite depth and nothing else' (*Building*, March 1939, p.118).

Meanwhile Skinner of Tecton brought back first-hand evidence from Barcelona. Tecton were working on a major plan for Finsbury – their Health Centre (figs 74 & 75) was a first fruit – and they embarked on a scientific study of effectively protecting the Borough against air raids. The government's solution was for countless small surface shelters, together with trenches and the use of existing basements. Tecton and Arup came down for deep bomb-proof shelters. Figure 124 shows their design for a massive multi-level shelter in Finsbury. 70 feet deep, for 7,600 people, it was circular in shape and rose spirally round a central services core. Asked, forty years later, if it was in fact built, Sir Ove Arup gently replied, 'Alas, the war came too soon.' But the concept was totally rejected by the government, and when a copy of Tecton's book, *Planned ARP*, which set out the scheme in detail, was sent to Winston Churchill it drew only a coldly snubbing rebuff.

By this time major commercial commissions often included provision against air attack. In 1938 McGrath designed a substantial factory for Aspro at Slough, though the war put a stop to its execution. Lavishly equipped, it included a small concert hall, a swimming pool, cricket, tennis and bowls pavilions, and also a sophisticated air raid shelter for 600 people, 7,000 square feet in area, with gas locks, filtration, sewage, and casualty wards. The gas locks are significant, for poison gas was a very real terror. Its use in the First World War led to a stream of prophetic novels, now totally forgotten, in the 20s and 30s, based on the annihilating horror of gas in the next war. For example in 1931 the popular novelist Neil Bell wrote *The Gas War of 1940* predicting scores of millions of victims next time round, and his book sold over 100,000 copies.

McGrath's sour family Christmas card (fig. 125) about this time needs no comment in itself, but it was not a new idea to him, for the design, without the seasonal greetings, had already been reproduced in his book of 1934, *Twentieth Century Houses*, with the caption, 'One possible use for the private house, a structure safe against air attack'.

Finis

On 25 May 1939 the *Architects' Journal* published 'Scoreboard', the result of a poll among 36 public figures, none of them architects, recording 'the six recent British buildings which they considered of the greatest merit'. The winner was Crabtree's Peter Jones; the runner-up Scott's Battersea Power Station. Tecton got the most votes, but Musman, Richardson, Lutyens, Comper were there too, as were H. J. Rowse and the architects to the Miners' Welfare Committee (and two Government Departments). Notable absentees were Lawn Road Flats, and any work by F.R.S. Yorke or Connell, Ward and Lucas.

But the coming war was now plainly in view and the decade's architectural work was almost over. Its architects were soon to be scattered into war work, many to fight, some into special fields like camouflage or rebuilding blitzed home industries, whilst older practitioners did what they could in a myriad humdrum jobs by day, and firewatched by night, looking on as the urban scene they had helped to shape was pounded and burnt. But the long years of the war, the professional frustrations, the huge potential of post-war Britain, the tidal wave of practical determination and social idealism undammed by the 1945 armistice, and what became of it all; that is another story.

Some Books on English Architecture, Design and the Environment published between 1930 and 1940

Patrick Abercrombie (ed.) *The Book of the modern house* 1939
M.H. Baillie Scott & A.E. Beresford *Houses and gardens* 1933
Anthony Bertram *The House: a machine for living in* 1935
Anthony Bertram *Design* 1938
Sir Reginald Blomfield *Modernismus* 1932
Geoffrey Boumphrey *Town and country tomorrow* 1940
Robert Byron *The Appreciation of architecture* 1932
Noel Carrington *Design in the home* 1933. Rev. ed. 1938
Noel Carrington *Design and a changing civilisation* 1935
Noel Carrington *The Shape of things* 1939
Ella Carter *Seaside houses and bungalows* 1939
John Gloag (ed.) *Design in modern life* 1934
Geoffrey Grigson (ed.) *The Arts today* 1935 (includes *Architecture* by John Summerson)
Alan Hastings (ed.) *Weekend houses, cottages and bungalows* 1939
C.G. Holme (ed.) *Industrial architecture* 1935
Raymond McGrath *Twentieth century houses* 1934
Duncan Miller *More colour schemes for the modern home* 1938
Museum of Modern Art (New York) *Modern architecture in England*. With essays by H-R. Hitchcock & Catherine K. Bauer 1937
Derek Patmore *Colour schemes for the modern home* 1933
Nikolaus Pevsner *An Enquiry into industrial art in England* 1937
R. Randal Phillips *Houses for moderate means* 1936. 2nd ed. 1939
Herbert Read (ed.) *Unit One* 1934
Herbert Read *Art and industry* 1934
C.H. Reilly *Scaffolding in the sky* 1938
RIBA *International architecture 1924-1934* (exhibition catalogue) 1934

RIBA *The Small house* (exhibition catalogue) 1938
J.M. Richards *An Introduction to modern architecture* 1940
Howard Robertson *Modern architectural design* 1932
Thomas Sharp *Town and countryside* 1932
Thomas Sharp *English panorama* 1936
Roger Smithells *Modern small country houses* 1936
Roger Smithells *The Country Life book of small houses* 1939
Roger Smithells & S. John Woods *The Modern home: its decoration, furnishing and equipment* 1936
John Summerson & Clough Williams-Ellis *Architecture here and now* 1934
The Studio Yearbook of decorative art. Annually
F.E. Towndrow *Architecture in the balance* 1933
Clough Williams-Ellis (ed.) *Britain and the beast* 1937
Myles Wright *Small houses £500 – £2500* 1937
F.R.S. Yorke *The Modern house in England* 1937
F.R.S. Yorke & Frederick Gibberd *The Modern flat* 1937
F.R.S. Yorke & Colin Penn *A Key to modern architecture* 1939

In addition, there are three important later sourcebooks:
Jeremy Gould *Modern houses in Britain, 1919-1939* 1979
(fully documented gazetteer, citing contemporary periodical references to over 900 houses)
Hampstead in the thirties: a committed decade. Exhibition catalogue. Camden Arts Centre 1974
Thirties: British art and design before the war. Exhibition catalogue. Arts Council 1979

Oliver Hill. Houses at Frinton (*see* p. 130)